The
Gulf Islands
Guide

**Salt Spring Island • Galiano Island
North and South Pender Islands
Mayne Island • Saturna Island**

Irene Rinn

Hillside Publishing

Canadian Cataloguing in Publication Data

Rinn, Irene.
The Gulf Islands guide

Includes index.
ISBN 0-9683132-0-5
1. Gulf Islands (B.C.)—Guidebooks. I. Title.
FC3845.G8R56 1998   917.11'2   C98-910554-7
F1089.G8R56 1998

Hillside Publishing
P.O. Box 45793
2397 King George Highway
Sunnyside Mall Post Office
Surrey, BC Canada
V4A 9N3
E-mail: irinn@earthlink.net

Distributed in Canada by
Gordon Soules Book Publishers Ltd.
1354-B Marine Drive
West Vancouver, BC V7T 1B5
(604) 922-6588 or (604) 688-5466
Fax: (604) 688-5442
E-mail: books@gordonsoules.com
Web site: http://www.gordonsoules.com

Distributed in the United States by
Gordon Soules Book Publishers Ltd.
620—1916 Pike Place
Seattle, WA 98101
Fax: (604) 688-5442
E-mail: books@gordonsoules.com
Web site: http://www.gordonsoules.com

Cover designed by Harry Bardal
Printed and bound in Canada by Hignell Printing Ltd.

CONTENTS

Acknowledgments

My thanks go to all who assisted me in compiling this guide.

Thanks go to Melanie Fewings for her skill and patience with the map art work and a job well done. Natalie Fewings deserves recognition for her research assistance and a memorable picnic at Winter Cove Park. Kudos go to Jody McBee for her unfailing support and encouragement all the way.

One of the many pleasures of writing this book has been meeting the photographers whose works depict the beauty of these islands. All have been generous with their time and have played an essential part in this book's development.

The countless others who have helped me with information also deserve a round of thanks. With their help, I offer this comprehensive guide to a captivating area— British Columbia's beautiful Gulf Islands.

For Natalie and Melanie,
the two great lights of my life.

Photo Credits

Note to the Reader

Information in any guidebook is subject to change and error. It is advisable to confirm information before travelling.

While great care has been taken to ensure the accuracy of the information in this book, neither the author nor the publisher can accept responsibility or liability for any outdated information, omissions, or errors. In addition, no omission should be taken as implying that any establishment or business is not reputable or worthy of inclusion in this book.

A listing of public access to beaches, docks, campgrounds, or other sites does not imply that such sites are safe for any particular activity. As well, some activities listed in this book could be dangerous. Readers should assure themselves of the safety of intended activities before entering any site or starting any activity or tour listed in this book.

FUTURE EDITIONS OF THIS BOOK

The author welcomes comments about this book and the information it contains. Corrections and clarifications are most welcome. Please send all information and suggestions to:

Irene Rinn
c/o Hillside Publishing
P.O. Box 45793
2397 King George Highway
Sunnyside Mall Post Office
Surrey, BC Canada
V4A 9N3
E-mail: irinn@earthlink.net

Introduction

Are you looking for a great getaway? Quick access to a rejuvenating weekend? A leave-it-all-behind vacation? The Gulf Islands are an ideal place to go.

The Gulf Islands are dotted along the protected waterway between mainland British Columbia and Vancouver Island. This book focuses on the six southern islands served by the British Columbia ferry system—Salt Spring, Galiano, North and South Pender, Mayne, and Saturna.

The many bays around the islands provide protected, spur-of-the-moment moorage for pleasure boaters. Orca whales, sea lions, and harbour seals live in the area. The entire coastline is a wonderland for boaters, kayakers, and canoeists.

Farmlands, ocean, and steep cliffs set the scene. Sheep and deer dot the fields. In season, there is a profusion of blooms—daffodils, daisies, foxglove, camas, and Dogwood trees. Quail cluck and deer browse among the ferns and the distinctive, twisted arbutus trees.

Sunny summer days and mild winters make the islands a destination for all seasons.

Explore the islands, savour their similarities and differences. Visit them all at once or on smaller excursions, taking day trips or weekend outings. Slow down, smell the flowers, and run on island time.

Highlights

Highlights common to all of these islands

tranquillity ... rustic charm ... quiet country atmosphere ... seascape views ... hiking ... cycling ... kayaking and canoeing ... ocean swimming ... beachcombing ... picnic spots ... boat charters ... scuba diving ... government docks ... galleries ... resorts ... restaurants ... pubs

Fulford Harbour viewed from Mount Maxwell.

Highlights of Salt Spring

largest of the islands ... the only island with a major town centre ... lake swimming ... bowling ... golfing ... tennis ... horseback riding ... hang gliding ... public swimming pool ... marinas ... petroglyph ... museum ... guided tours ... artists' and artisans' home studios ... festival of the arts ... fall fair ... wine festival ... jazz festival ... summerlong sale of pottery, art, jewelry ... artisans' Christmas show and sale ... farmers' market ... hostel ... inns ... cottages ... hotels ... motels ... bed and breakfasts ... oceanside and forest campgrounds

Highlights of Galiano

easiest access from mainland B.C. ... golfing ... horseback riding ... marina ... artists' and artisans' home studios ... summer fair ... blackberry festival ... weavers' and spinners' sale ... lodges ... inns ... bed and breakfasts ... campgrounds ... bus for boaters

Highlights of North and South Pender

lake swimming ... golfing ... tennis ... marinas ... boaters' port of entry with waterside lounge and pool ... divers' lodge ... fall fair ... historic store ... farmers' market ... lodges ... inns ... bed and breakfasts ... campgrounds

Highlights of Mayne

tennis ... lightstation ... museum ... salmon derby ... fall fair ... Christmas craft fair ... old-fashioned general store ... lodges ... inns ... bed and breakfasts ... campgrounds

Highlights of Saturna
least developed of all the islands ... farm bakery ... lodges

Getting to the Gulf Islands by ferry

The maps in this book give routes and port-to-port names. Information on getting to the individual islands is in the section for each island.

For assured boarding with a vehicle on the Tsawwassen-Gulf Islands ferries, reservations are highly recommended and can be made at no extra cost. Reservations on the Tsawwassen to Swartz Bay route can be made for a fee. Boarding on all other routes is first come, first served.

Groups of fifteen or more people in one vehicle or walking on in a group (bicycles included) can make a reservation on any route. Group rates are available if reservations are made seven days in advance.

Ferries meeting in Active Pass.

It is difficult to get on and off some islands in one day, especially if you arrive late in the day. As accommodation on the islands is limited, it is wise to plan your arrival, departure, and accommodation before setting out.

Getting to the Gulf Islands from the B.C. mainland by B.C. Ferries
1. Tsawwassen, 37 kilometres (about forty minutes) southwest of Vancouver on Highway 17, is the departure point for traveling directly to the Gulf Islands. Sail

directly to the island of your choice or sail from Tsawwassen to Swartz Bay (an hour and a half) and transfer to sail to the island you choose. Reservations can be made on the Tsawwassen to Gulf Islands routes only.

2. Horseshoe Bay, 23 kilometres (about thirty-five minutes) north of Vancouver, is the departure point to Departure Bay, near Nanaimo on Vancouver Island. Sailing time is one hour and thirty-five minutes. There are two choices from Departure Bay:
- Drive 42 kilometres (thirty-five minutes) south to Crofton and take a twenty-minute ferry to Vesuvius Bay on Salt Spring Island. The other Gulf Islands can be reached from Long Harbour on Salt Spring.
- Drive 132 kilometres (two and a half hours) to Swartz Bay and take a ferry to the island of your choice.

Getting to the Gulf Islands from Vancouver Island by B.C. Ferries
1. Swartz Bay, 30 kilometres (forty minutes) north of Victoria, is the main ferry terminal. Sail to any of the islands from there.
2. Crofton, 80 kilometres (an hour and a quarter) north of Victoria, is a departure point for Salt Spring Island. Sailing time is twenty minutes.

B.C. Ferries schedule information and reservations
British Columbia Ferries
1112 Fort Street
Victoria, BC V8V 4V2
Web site: http://www.bcferries.bc.ca
In British Columbia: 1-888-223-3779
Outside British Columbia: 250-386-3431
B.C. Ferries accepts Visa and MasterCard for phone reservations and Visa, MasterCard, and Canadian and American currency at all ferry terminals. There are ATM machines and a currency exchange at the Tsawwassen terminal.

Getting to the Gulf Islands from the United States
1. From Tsawwassen, B.C., by B.C. Ferries: Drive to Tsawwassen, 230 kilometres north of Seattle, on Interstate Highway 5 and, in Canada, on Highways 99 and 17. Take the ferry directly to the Gulf Island of your choice, or take the ferry from Tsawwassen to Swartz Bay on Vancouver Island (one and a half hours) and then transfer to the ferry to the island of your choice. Reservations can be made for ferries from Tsawwassen to the Gulf Islands. No reservations can be made for ferries from Swartz Bay to the Gulf Islands. Food service Tsawwassen to Gulf Islands.

B.C. Ferries schedule information and reservations
British Columbia Ferries
1112 Fort Street
Victoria, BC V8V 4V2
Web site: http://www.bcferries.bc.ca
In British Columbia: 1-888-223-3779
Outside British Columbia: 250-386-3431

B.C. Ferries accepts Visa and MasterCard for phone reservations and Visa, Master-Card, and Canadian and American currency at all ferry terminals. There are ATM machines and a currency exchange at the Tsawwassen terminal.

2. From Anacortes, Washington, by the Washington State ferry system: Drive to

Bennett Bay and Mount Baker.

Anacortes (85 miles north and 20 miles west of Seattle) and take the ferry to Sidney, B.C. Sailing time is three hours. Reservations taken. Food service. From Sidney, drive 8 kilometres (fifteen minutes) to the B.C. Ferries terminal at Swartz Bay and take the ferry to the island of your choice.

Washington State Ferries schedule information and reservations
Washington State Ferries
Pier 52
801 Alaskan Way
Seattle, WA 98104-1487
E-mail: wsf@wsdot.wa.gov
Web site: http://www.wsdot.wa.gov/ferries/
In U.S.: 1-800-843-3779
Outside U.S.: 206-464-6400

3. From Seattle, Washington, by the Princess Marguerite (Clipper Navigation): Sail from Seattle to Victoria, B.C. Sailing time is four and a half hours. Reservations can be made. Food service. From Victoria, drive 30 kilometres (forty-five minutes) to the B.C. Ferries terminal at Swartz Bay and take a ferry to the island of your choice.

Clipper Navigation schedule information and reservations
Clipper Navigation
2701 Alaskan Way
Pier 69
Seattle, WA 98121
E-mail: clipper@nwlink.com
Web site: http://www.victoriaclipper.com/
In U.S.: 1-800-888-2535
Outside U.S.: 206-448-5000

4. From Port Angeles, Washington (on the Olympic Peninsula), by Black Ball Transport ferry: Drive to Port Angeles and sail on the Black Ball Transport ferry to Victoria, B.C. Sailing time is an hour and a half. No reservations can be made. Food service. From Victoria, drive 30 kilometres (forty-five minutes) to the B.C. Ferries terminal at Swartz Bay and take a ferry to the island of your choice.

Black Ball Transport ferry schedule information and reservations
Black Ball Transport
430 Belleville Street
Victoria, BC V8V 1W9
Web site: http://www.northolympic.com/coho
In U.S.: 306-457-4491
In Canada: 250-386-2202

Getting to the Gulf Islands by air

Hanna Air: Charter flights between all the Gulf Islands and Vancouver. 250-537-9359 or 1-800-665-2FLY (in B.C.). Fax: 250-247-8303.

Harbour Air: Daily seaplane service between downtown Vancouver or the Vancouver airport and Salt Spring, Galiano, Saturna, North Pender, and Mayne islands. Also charter service. 604-688-1277 or 250-537-5525 or 1-800-665-0212 (in Canada and the U.S.).

Seair: Daily flights from Vancouver airport to Galiano, Saturna, Pender, and Mayne islands. Also charter service. 604-273-8900 or 1-800-447-3247 (in B.C.).

Accommodation on the islands

Reservations are highly recommended, especially during summer months, weekends, and holidays, because facilities are limited and many places are closed in the off-season. The full range of accommodation offers something for every budget. Refer to *Accommodations*, a free annual publication by the B.C. government, available at Travel InfoCentres throughout the province or by calling

Ministry of Tourism
Travel Reservation and Information Service
In Greater Vancouver: 663-6000
In North America, outside Greater Vancouver: 1-800-663-6000
Outside North America: 250-387-1642
Web site: http://www.tbc.gov.bc.ca/tourism/information.html

Other resources

Canadian Gulf Islands Reservation Service
637 Southwind Road
Galiano Island, BC V0N 1P0
250-539-5390 Fax: 250-539-5390
E-mail: reservations@gulfislands.com
Web site: http://www.multimedia.bcit.bc.ca/b&b

Island Escapades Adventures
118 Natalie Lane
Ganges, BC V8K 2C6
250-537-2537 Fax: 250-537-2532

Salt Spring Sojourn
221 Langs Road
Salt Spring Island, BC V8K 1N3
250-537-0753 or 250-537-2868
E-mail: saltspring@islandnet.com
Web site: http://www.islandnet.com/saltspring/

Salt Spring Vacation Rentals
P.O. Box 818
Ganges, BC V8K 2W3
250-537-9108 or 1-888-280-7787
E-mail: vacation@saltspring.com
Web site: http://www.vacations.bc.ca

British Columbia Bed and Breakfast Association
101—1001 West Broadway
Vancouver, BC V6H 4V1
604-734-3486 Fax: 604-985-6037

Salt Spring Island Visitor Information Centre
P.O. Box 111
Ganges, BC V8K 2T1
250-537-5252 Fax: 250-537-4276

Seal on log.

E-mail: chamber@saltspring.com
Web site: http://www.saltspringisland.bc.ca

Galiano Island Travel InfoCentre
P.O. Box 73
Galiano Island, BC V0N 1P0
250-539-2233 Fax: 250-539-2233
Web site: http://www.islandnet.com/galiano

Mayne Island Chamber of Commerce
P.O. Box 160
Mayne Island, BC V0N 2J0
No telephone service

Other information
Current happenings and services
Each island's newspaper is a good source of information on current happenings and services.

Listings of B.C.'s marine parks
B.C. Parks

4000 Seymour Place
Victoria, BC V8V 1X5
250-387-4363

Canadian hydrographic service charts
Institute of Ocean Sciences
P.O. Box 6000
Sidney, BC V8L 4B2
250-363-6358

Weather information
Environment Canada marine weather (recorded message): 250-656-2714
Canadian Coast Guard marine report (recorded message): 604-666-3655

Tidal information
Institute of Ocean Sciences as above

Border crossing and duty information
Revenue Canada Customs and Excise
333 Dunsmuir Street
Vancouver, BC V6B 5R4
604-666-0545

Canada Customs office on Pender Island
250-629-3363 (May through September)

The metric system
Canada uses the metric system. Here are some handy tips for visitors unfamiliar
with the system:

One kilometre equals .62 miles. Multiply kilometres by .62 to convert to miles.

Speed limit calculation tip: Drop the zero on the posted speed, multiply by six and
you have an approximation of the speed limit in miles per hour. Example: 80 kilometres per hour equals 8 x 6 equals 48 miles per hour.

Celsius to Fahrenheit: Multiply the temperature in Celsius by 1.8 and add 32.

Gasoline is sold by the litre: 3.78 litres equals one U.S. gallon.

One kilogram equals 2.2 pounds
500 grams equals about one pound
One metre equals 39 inches
One centimetre equals .4 inches
One hectare equals 2.5 acres

Chapter One

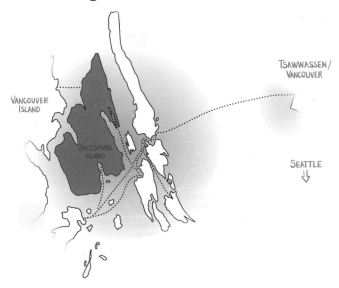

Salt Spring Island

largest of the islands • the only island with a major town centre • tranquillity • rustic charm • quiet country atmosphere • seascape views • hiking • cycling • kayaking and canoeing • ocean swimming • lake swimming • beachcombing • picnic spots • boat charters • scuba diving • bowling • golfing • tennis • horseback riding • hang gliding • public swimming pool • government docks • marinas • petroglyph • museum • guided tours • galleries • artists' and artisans' home studios • festival of the arts • fall fair wine festival • jazz festival • summer-long sale of pottery, art, jewelry • artisans' Christmas show and sale • farmers' market • hostel • resorts • inns • cottages • hotels • motels • bed and breakfasts • oceanside and forest campgrounds • restaurants • pubs

Salt Spring Island, located between the other Gulf Islands and southern Vancouver Island, is about 12 kilometres in length and ranges topographically from rocky inlets through the meadows of Fulford Valley to the tops of Mounts Bruce, Tuam, and Maxwell.

The largest and most developed of the islands, Salt Spring has a population of about ten thousand.

Sheep at Ruckle Park.

Getting to Salt Spring by ferry

Getting to Salt Spring from the B.C. mainland by B.C. Ferries

1. Tsawwassen to Long Harbour on Salt Spring Island: This is the most direct route from the mainland to Salt Spring Island. Tsawwassen is 37 kilometres (about forty minutes) southwest of Vancouver on Highway 17. Long Harbour is 5 kilometres from Ganges, the largest town on the island. Sailing time is about two and a half hours. Check the schedule for details. Reservations can be made. Food service.

2. From Tsawwassen to Swartz Bay on Vancouver Island and from Swartz Bay to Fulford Harbour on Salt Spring Island: Sailing time totals about two hours. Check the schedule for details. Ask the cashier for a transfer. No reservations can be made. Food service on the Tsawwassen to Swartz Bay route.

3. From Horseshoe Bay to Departure Bay (Nanaimo) on Vancouver Island, from Departure Bay to Crofton, and from Crofton to Vesuvius on Salt Spring Island: Horseshoe Bay is 23 kilometres (about thirty-five minutes) north of Vancouver. Sailing time from Horseshoe Bay to Departure Bay is about an hour and a half. From Nanaimo, drive 42 kilometres (thirty-five minutes) south to the Crofton ferry terminal and sail for twenty minutes to Vesuvius on Salt Spring Island. Reservations taken and food service on the Horseshoe Bay to Departure Bay route.

Getting to Salt Spring from Vancouver Island by B.C. Ferries

1. Swartz Bay to Fulford Harbour on Salt Spring Island: Swartz Bay is on Vancouver Island, 30 kilometres (forty-five minutes) north of Victoria. Sailing time is about thir-

ty-five minutes. Ferries go approximately every hour and a half. No reservations can be made. No food service.

2. Crofton to Vesuvius Bay on Salt Spring Island: Crofton is 80 kilometres north of Victoria. Sailing time is twenty minutes. No reservations can be made. No food service.

B.C. Ferries schedule information and reservations
British Columbia Ferries
1112 Fort Street
Victoria, BC V8V 4V2
Web site: http://www.bcferries.bc.ca
In British Columbia: 1-888-223-3779
Outside British Columbia: 250-386-3431

Getting to Salt Spring from the United States
1. From Tsawwassen, B.C., by B.C. Ferries: Drive to Tsawwassen, 230 kilometres north of Seattle, on Interstate Highway 5 and, in Canada, Highways 99 and 17. Take the ferry directly to Long Harbour on Salt Spring Island, or take the ferry from Tsawwassen to Swartz Bay on Vancouver Island (one and a half hours) and then transfer to the ferry to Fulford Harbour on Salt Sping Island. Reservations can be made for ferries from Tsawwassen to Salt Spring. No reservations can be made for ferries from Swartz Bay to Salt Spring. Food service Tsawwassen to Salt Spring.

B.C. Ferries schedule information and reservations
British Columbia Ferries
1112 Fort Street
Victoria, BC V8V 4V2
Web site: http://www.bcferries.bc.ca
In British Columbia: 1-888-223-3779
Outside British Columbia: 250-386-3431
    B.C. Ferries accepts Visa and MasterCard for phone reservations and Visa, MasterCard, and Canadian and American currency at all ferry terminals. There are ATM machines and a currency exchange at the Tsawwassen terminal.

2. From Anacortes, Washington by the Washington State ferry system: Drive to Anacortes (85 miles north and 20 miles west of Seattle) and take the ferry to Sidney, B.C. Sailing time is three hours. Reservations taken. Food service. From Sidney, drive 8 kilometres (fifteen minutes) to the B.C. Ferries terminal at Swartz Bay and take the ferry to Fulford Harbour on Salt Spring Island.

Washington State Ferries schedule information and reservations
Washington State Ferries
Pier 52
801 Alaskan Way
Seattle, WA 98104-1487

E-mail: wsf@wsdot.wa.gov
Web site: http://www.wsdot.wa.gov/ferries/
In U.S.: 1-800-843-3779
Outside U.S.: 206-464-6400

3. From Seattle, Washington, by the Princess Marguerite (Clipper Navigation): Sail from Seattle to Victoria, B.C. Sailing time is four and a half hours. Reservations can be made. Food service. From Victoria, drive 30 kilometres (forty-five minutes) to the B.C. Ferries terminal at Swartz Bay and take the ferry to Fulford Harbour on Salt Spring Island.

Clipper Navigation schedule information and reservations
Clipper Navigation
2701 Alaskan Way
Pier 69
Seattle, WA 98121
E-mail: clipper@nwlink.com
Web site: http://www.victoriaclipper.com/
In U.S.: 1-800-888-2535
Outside U.S.: 206-448-5000

4. From Port Angeles, Washington (on the Olympic Peninsula) by Black Ball Transport ferry: Drive to Port Angeles and sail on the Black Ball Transport ferry to Victoria, B.C. Sailing time is an hour and a half. No reservations can be made. Food service. From Victoria, drive 30 kilometres (forty-five minutes) to the B.C. Ferries terminal at Swartz Bay and take the ferry to Salt Spring Island.

Black Ball Transport ferry schedule information and reservations
Black Ball Transport
430 Belleville Street
Victoria, BC V8V 1W9
Web site: http://www.northolympic.com/coho
In U.S.: 360-457-4491
In Canada: 250-386-2202

Accommodation

Plan ahead for accommodation; facilities are limited and heavily booked at the height of the tourist season, and some are closed in the off-season. The Salt Spring Chamber of Commerce produces an annual list of accommodation of all kinds—hotels, motels, hostels, resorts, traditional and self-contained bed and breakfasts, and rental cottages. The list is available at the Tourist InfoCentre at P.O. Box 111, Ganges, BC, V0S 1E0. 250-537-5252. Fax: 250-537-4276.

Other resources

Island Escapades Adventures
118 Natalie Lane
Ganges, BC V8K 2C6
250-537-2537 Fax: 250-537-2532

Salt Spring Sojourn
221 Langs Road
Salt Spring Island, BC V8K 1N3
250-537-0753 or 250-537-2868
E-mail: saltspring@islandnet.com
Web site: http://www.islandnet.com/saltspring/

Salt Spring Vacation Rentals
P.O. Box 818
Ganges, BC V8K 2W3
250-537-9108 or 1-888-280-7787
E-mail: vacation@saltspring.com
Web site: http://www.vacations.bc.ca

Canadian Gulf Islands Reservation Service
637 Southwind Road
Galiano Island, BC V0N 1P0
250-539-5390 Fax: 250-539-5390
E-mail: reservations@gulfislands.com
Web site: http://www.multimedia.bcit.bc.ca/b&b

British Columbia Bed and Breakfast Association
101—1001 West Broadway
Vancouver, BC V6H 4V1
604-734-3486 Fax: 604-985-6037

Ministry of Tourism
Travel Reservation and Information Service
In Greater Vancouver: 663-6000
In North America, outside Greater Vancouver: 1-800-663-6000
Outside North America: 250-387-1642
Web site: http://www.tbc.gov.bc.ca/tourism/information.html

Hostels

Salt Spring Island Hostel: 640 Cusheon Lake Road. Budget, dormitory-style accommodation on ten forested acres. Tepees and a tree house. Rate includes use of kitchen and living room. Short walk to lake and ocean. Bike rentals. 250-537-4149.
E-mail: mike@raven.bc.ca

Resorts, inns, cottages, hotels, motels

There are no restaurants on the premises in the following listings unless mentioned.

Beachcomber: 770 Vesuvius Bay Road. Large kitchen and sleeping units overlooking the ocean or orchard. Near golf, tennis, public pool, beach, store. Walking distance to Vesuvius-Crofton (Vancouver Island) ferry, Vesuvius Beach, Vesuvius Pub, and Seaside Kitchen. 250-537-5415.

Cedar Beach Resort: 1136 North End Road. On St. Mary Lake. One- and two-bedroom units, fully equipped cedar cabins, and motel rooms. On six acres, amid tall stands of cedar. Lake swimming, outdoor pool, hot tub, sauna. Badminton, tetherball, horseshoes. Fishing in season. Canoes, rowboats, kayaks. Conference facilities. Accommodation for people with disabilities. 1-800-562-3327 in B.C. or 250-537-2205. Fax: 250-537-1118.

Cottage Resort: 175 Suffolk Road. Five and a half acres on the south end of St. Mary Lake. Cabins with fully equipped kitchens and TVs. Some fireplaces. Boats, swimming, fishing, sandy beach. Complimentary rowboats and canoes. English country gardens. Near golf course and tennis. 250-537-2214.

Cusheon Lake Resort: 171 Natalie Lane. Quiet, sheltered area on Cusheon Lake. Log and A-frame chalets, most with fireplaces. Fully equipped kitchens, outdoor hot tub overlooking lake, barbecue, swimming, boats, fishing. 250-537-9629. Fax: 250-537-9629.

Fulford Inn: 2661 Fulford-Ganges Road at Fulford Harbour. Rooms with harbour view. Bed and breakfast rates. Children welcome. Restaurant and pub with fireplace. 250-653-4432. Fax: 250-653-4331.

Fulford Inn.

Green Acres Resort: 241 Langs Road. Twelve fully equipped one- or two-bedroom lakefront cottages, all with fireplaces. Cablevision. Lake swimming. Complimentary rowboats, paddle boats, and canoes. Propane barbecues and firewood. Trophy fishing, tackle, bait. Playground and sandy beach. Family oriented. 1-800-667-0774 or 250-537-2585. Fax: 250-537-9901.

Harbour House Hotel: 121 Upper Ganges Road. Across from the harbour at Ganges. Some units with balconies. Restaurant, pub, beer and wine store. Seminar and banquet facilities. Short walk to downtown. 250-537-5571. Fax: 250-537-4618.

Hastings House: 160 Upper Ganges Road. Upscale lodging in a seaside farm estate overlooking Ganges Harbour. Winner of awards as a prestigious North American getaway. Spacious character cottages. Two dining rooms (one formal, one informal) in elegant, tudor-style manor house. Breakfast and tea included. Small conference facility. Licensed. 1-800-661-9255 in Canada and the U.S. or 250-537-2362. Fax: 250-537-5333.

Lakeside Gardens Resort: 1450 North End Road. At the northeast end of St. Mary Lake. Family oriented. Fully equipped panabode cabins with fireplaces. Campsites with fire pits on the lakeshore. Showers. Boat rentals. Sandy beach, swimming. Bass and trout fishing. 250-537-5773.

Maple Ridge Cottages: 301 Tripp Road. Fully equipped cottages on St. Mary Lake. Queen-sized beds, sun decks, barbecues. Swimming, fishing. Complimentary canoes, rowboats, windsurfers, sailboat. Ferry pick-up. Near golf and tennis. 250-537-5977.

Salty Springs Spa Resort: 1460 North Beach Road. Ten chalets and two cabins, all with fireplaces, gas barbecues, fully equipped kitchens. Two-person mineral bath with seventy airjets and natural mineral water in each chalet. Spa. Shiatsu aromatherapy and hydrotherapy. Games room. Complimentary rowboats and mountain bikes. 250-537-4111. Fax: 250-537-2939.

Seabreeze Inn: 101 Bittancourt Road. Off Fulford Ganges Road about 1 kilometre south of Ganges. Twenty-eight units, some with kitchenettes. Short walk to facilities and shopping in Ganges. 1-800-434-4112 in Canada and U.S. or 250-537-4145. Fax: 250-537-4323.

Spindrift Resort: 255 Welbury Point (near the Long Harbour ferry terminal). Six cottages on a six-acre peninsula, amid arbutus groves. Cottages with fireplaces directly overlook the sea. Wildlife. Private white sand beaches. Quiet pets welcome. Small resort suited to adults who want quiet relaxation in a secluded environment. 250-537-5311.

St. Mary Lake Resort: 1170 North End Road. One- or two-bedroom housekeeping units with kitchens and fireplaces. Sandy swimming beach. Fishing. Playground. Complimentary rowboats and canoes. Family oriented. 250-537-2832.

Bed and breakfasts

Treat yourself to a stay at one of the many bed and breakfasts on the island. Roadside signs make most easy to find, but calling ahead is strongly recommended. A list of names and phone numbers is available from the Travel InfoCentre in Ganges. Some bed and breakfasts open year-round are:

Eagle and seagulls.

Beach House at Fulford Harbour: 369 Isabella Point Road. Peaceful and secluded. Self-contained one-bedroom suite with kitchen and oceanside deck. Two new beach-front guestrooms, one with Jacuzzi. Private baths and entrances. Fireplaces. Beverage bar, laundry, barbecue. Steps to tidal beach. Crabbing, beachcombing. 250-653-2040. Fax: 250-653-9711.

Beach House on Sunset Drive: 930 Sunset Drive. Five acres of gardens on 1000 feet of private waterfront. Large ocean suites with private entrances, balconies, bathrobes, and fresh fruit trays. Self-contained one-bedroom cottages with ocean view and private baths. Full gourmet breakfast included. Adult oriented. 250-537-2879. Fax: 250-537-4747.

Captain's Hideaway: 162 Harrison Avenue. Tidal waterfront on Booth Inlet. Self-contained suite with kitchen, den, and bathroom. 250-537-9595.

Cranberry Ridge: 269 Don Ore Road. Three tastefully decorated rooms in house designed to be a B&B. Ensuite plus Jacuzzi. One room with fireplace. Large sun deck with six- to eight-person hot tub overlooking magnificent ocean view. Healthy breakfasts. Two kilometres south of Ganges. 250-537-4854.

Heathers Hollow: 121 Central Avenue. Contemporary log house on nine secluded wooded acres. Half a kilometre from the Long Harbour ferry terminal. Down duvets. Organic vegetarian breakfasts. 250-537-5180. Fax: 250-537-5180.

Pomodori: 375 Baker Road at Booth Bay. Seaside accommodation in a house built in 1911. Two rooms on the ocean. Shared bath. Antique furnishings. Two patios overlooking the ocean. Two dining rooms with fireplaces. 250-537-2247.

The White Fig: 135 Goodrich Road. Near Vesuvius Bay. Oceanview cottage and guest rooms. Antiques, private entrances, patios, fireplaces, sun deck. Gourmet breakfast. Walk to beach, pub, and ferry. 250-537-5791.

Water's Edge: 327 Price Road. Seaview guest room suites. Fridge, light cooking. Waterside guest sitting room and suites. Fireplace. Delicious breakfast on covered patio or indoors. Rowboating, beachcombing, country gardens. 250-537-5807. Fax: 250-537-2862.

Weston Lake Inn: 813 Beaver Point Road. Secluded country getaway on ten acres. Overlooks Weston Lake. Lovely rooms with down quilts. Satellite TV and carefully prepared breakfasts. Fireside lounge with library, games, movies. Private baths. Outdoor hot tub. Adult oriented, non-smoking. 250-653-4311.

Wisteria Guest House: 268 Park Drive. Quiet retreat on an acre of gardens. Six rooms and one cottage. Two blocks from downtown and marina. Bedrooms with adjoining baths. Large lounge with fireplace. Accommodates seminars, reunions, weddings. Ferry pick-up. 250-537-5899.

Campgrounds

Lakeside Gardens Resort: 1450 North End Road. On the northeast end of St. Mary Lake. Campsites, cabanas with outdoor cooking facilities, cottages, RV accommodation. Boat rentals, fire pits, showers. 250-537-5773.

Mouat Park: Public park in Ganges at the end of Seaview Avenue. Fifteen drive-in sites amid cedars and ferns. Four walk-in or cycle-in sites. Easy walking to downtown Ganges. Open year round. No RV hook-ups.

Ruckle Park: Public park at the southern tip of the island. Seventy walk-in campsites, some on the shoreline with close-up views of passing ferries. Some group sites. Reservations can be made only for large group camping. 250-653-4115 and 250-539-2115.

Salt Spring Island Hostel: 640 Cusheon Lake Road. Tent sites available at hostel on 10 acres near lake and ocean. 250-537-4149.
E-mail: mike@raven.bc.ca

Ferry and tents at Ruckle Park.

Restaurants, pubs, and take-out food

Restaurants are listed by proximity to Ganges, Fulford Harbour, or Vesuvius. Mouat's Mall and Grace Point Square are in the centre of Ganges at the waterfront on Ganges Harbour. Creekside is on McPhillips Avenue. Gasoline Alley is beside Centennial Park in the centre of Ganges. The Upper Ganges Centre is on Lower Ganges Road north of Ganges.

Restaurants and pubs in or near Ganges

Alfresco Restaurant and Café: In Grace Point Square. Restaurant specializes in pasta, seafood, and lamb dishes. Waterfront dining. Outdoor patio. Downstairs café with cappuccino, homemade soups, salads, sandwiches, and desserts. Licensed. 250-537-5979.

Barb's Buns: In Creekside building. Soups, sandwiches, pastries, vegetarian lunches, whole grain breads, bagels, cookies, and more. 250-537-4491.

Bouzouki Greek Café: In Grace Point Square. Waterfront dining with patio. Authentic Greek cuisine, home-baked desserts. Lunch and dinner. Licensed. Wheelchair accessible. 250-537-4181.

Crescent Moon Vegetarian Café: On Hereford Avenue, one block from the Travel InfoCentre. Organic vegetarian food. Fresh juice bar. Mexican menu. Italian ice cream. 250-537-1960.

Dagwood's Diner: In Upper Ganges Centre. Breakfast, gourmet burgers, English fish and chips, pizza. Full take-out menu. Indoor and patio seating. Licensed. 250-537-9323.

Dairy Queen/Orange Julius: In the Thrifty Foods building in the centre of Ganges. Family restaurant. 250-537-4447.

Golden Island Chinese Restaurant: In Upper Ganges Centre. Eat-in or take-out Chinese food. Air conditioned. Licensed. 250-537-2535.

Harbour House Bistro: At the Harbour House Hotel at the head of Ganges harbour. Open for lunch and dinner. Breakfast on weekends. Picturesque harbour view. Outdoor patio. Licensed. 250-537-4700.

Hastings House: 160 Upper Ganges Road. Two dining rooms, one formal, one informal. Upscale dining in an old farmhouse. Award-winning getaway setting and cuisine. Sunday brunch through the summer. Reservations required for lunch and dinner. Licensed. 1-800-661-9255 or 250-537-2362.

HMS *Ganges* Lounge: In the Harbour House Hotel on Ganges harbour. Authentic English pub menu. Deck dining with oceanview. Weekend entertainment. 250-537-5571.

House Piccolo: 108 Hereford Avenue near the Tourist InfoCentre. Gourmet Scandinavian and European cuisine. Reservations recommended. Licensed. 250-537-1844.

Ingle's Family Restaurant: 133 Lower Ganges Road. Family restaurant with salad bar and children's menu. Patio dining overlooking Ganges Harbour. Licensed. 250-537-4127.

Kanaka Restaurant: In Harbour Building in the centre of Ganges. European-style family restaurant. Breakfast, lunch, and dinner. Salt Spring Island lamb, fresh seafood. Patio dining. Coffee shop and dining room overlooking the harbour. Air conditioned. Licensed. 250-537-5041.

Kings Lane: 154 Kings Lane (at the bowling alley). Deli, soups, fish and chips, burgers. Breakfast, lunch, and dinner. 250-537-2054.

Maxine's Boardwalk Café: Dockside at Mouat's Mall. Outdoor patio. Overlooks Ganges' inner harbour. Pacific West Coast cuisine. Natural food, with vegetarian selections. Breakfast and lunch. Licensed. 250-537-5747.

Moby's Marine Pub: 124 Upper Ganges Road (at north end of Ganges Harbour). Deck dining looking onto the harbour. Marine pub with full dining menu and seafood and vegetarian specialties. Kitchen open until midnight seven days a week. Weekend brunch. Live entertainment. Gift shop, laundromat, showers. Licensed. 250-537-5559.

Mulligan's at the Club: 805 Lower Ganges Road at the golf course. Open to the public. 250-537-1760.

Pomodori: 375 Baker Road at Booth Bay. Bayside dining in a house built in 1911. Two dining rooms with fireplaces. Mediterranean and West Coast cuisine. Vegetarian, seafood, and pasta dishes. Local lamb. Homemade bread and desserts. Licensed. 250-537-2247.

Salt Spring Roasting Company: On McPhillips Avenue in the centre of Ganges. Fresh Arabica coffee roasted on the premises. Homemade soups and breads, Panini sandwiches, and desserts. Quality teas, chai, fresh-squeezed juices. 250-537-0825.

Seacourt Restaurant: Next to Centennial Park. Oceanfront dining. Classic Continental and Thai cuisine. Dining room and patio seating. Outdoor barbecue in summer. Licensed. 250-537-4611.

Sweet Arts Patisserie and Café: In Upper Ganges Centre. Breakfast and lunch specials. Specialty breads and sandwiches. Cappuccino, latte, espresso. Homemade desserts and delicious treats. 250-537-4205.

Tides Inn Restaurant: 132 Lower Ganges Road. Features local produce, seafood, lamb. Family restaurant. Licensed. 250-537-1097.

Tree House Café: On McPhillips Avenue in the centre of Ganges. Specialty sandwiches, tofu, soups, and pastries. Espresso. Outside tables. Live music. 250-537-5379.

Twisters: In Gasoline Alley next to Centennial Park. Family restaurant. Burgers, sandwiches. Breakfast all day. 250-537-4414.

Take-out food in Ganges

Alfresco to Go: Beside the harbour at Rainbow Road. Soups, submarines, large selection of take-out entrées, Italian ice creams. 250-537-0082.

Fulford Post Office and Rodrigo's Restaurant.

Barb's Buns: In Creekside building on McPhillips Avenue. Whole grain breads and pastries. Organic coffee. 250-537-4491.

Canadian 2 For 1 Pizza: 370 Lower Ganges Road. In the Upper Ganges Centre, next to Ganges Village Market. Pizza, chicken, ribs, pasta, salads. Pick-up or delivery. 250-537-5552.

Dagwood's Diner: In Upper Ganges Centre. Gourmet burgers, English fish and chips. Licensed. 250-537-9323.

Embe Bakery: At the base of Ganges hill, on the south edge of town. Breads and baked treats, soup, chili, sandwiches, coffee. Open early. 250-537-5611.

Glad's Ice Cream and Goodies: In Ganges, beside Mouat's Mall. Ice cream, waffle cones, fruit yogurt, muffins, and cookies. 250-537-4211.

Golden Island Chinese Restaurant: In the Upper Ganges Centre. Chinese food. 250-537-2535.

Harlan's Chocolate Treats: Across from Centennial Park in the centre of Ganges. Ice cream, fresh fruit frozen yogurt, hand-dipped Belgian chocolate truffles, fresh roasted coffees and teas. 250-537-4434.

Moby's Marine Pub: 120 Upper Ganges Road. Take-out menu. 250-537-5559.

Seacourt Restaurant: 149 Fulford Ganges Road (next to Centennial Park). Continental and Thai cuisine. 250-537-4611.

Restaurants, pubs, and take-out food in or near Fulford Harbour

The Blue Heron Family Restaurant: In the Fulford Inn on Fulford Harbour. Dining room and pub with fireplace. Salt Spring lamb and local seafood. Lunches on the patio. Sunday brunch. Licensed. 250-653-4432.

Rodrigo's Restaurant: At the ferry dock. Casual dining. Hearty soups, Mexican food, home-cooked pies. Licensed. 250-653-9222.

Sargeant's Mercantile: At Fulford Marina. Fresh produce and meat, in-store bakery, gourmet pizza, deli diner. 250-653-9600.

Salt Spring Roasting Company: Near the ferry dock. Fresh Arabica coffee roasted on the premises. Homemade soups and breads, Panini sandwiches, and desserts. Quality teas, chai, fresh-squeezed juices. 250-537-0825.

Restaurants, pubs, and take-out food in or near Vesuvius

Seaside Kitchen: 795 Vesuvius Bay Road. Casual dining overlooking the water and close to the ferry. Take-out window as well. Licensed. 250-537-2249.

Vesuvius Inn: At the ferry terminal. Substantial food in a neighbourhood pub overlooking Stuart Channel. Fireside and deck dining with a view. Live entertainment. Library/games room, dart room. No minors. Licensed. 250-537-2312.

Activities

Cycling

Cycling is a favoured activity for visitors and is an excellent way to enjoy the island. However, cyclists and motorists alike must exercise caution as the roads are winding, narrow, and mainly without cycle paths. There are both paved and gravel roads, with considerable variations in degree of difficulty.

One popular route is to begin at Ganges, go toward the north end of the island on Lower Ganges and North End roads, and return via Sunset Drive, which is a paved road with shoulders for cycle paths for a short distance. This route takes you past Portlock Park, with its public pool and playground, tennis courts, and picnic tables, and past St. Mary Lake, the rolling farmland on Sunset Drive, and the small village of Vesuvius with its country store and welcoming inn.

Another very popular route is through the Fulford Valley to Beaver Point. The distance from Ganges to Beaver Point is about 24 kilometres. There are two large hills—one just south of Ganges and one near Fulford Valley.

See the Loop Route section for suggested routes describing views and points of interest.

Cycling supplies, rentals, repairs

Bicycle Bob's: 324 Lower Ganges Road. Bicycle repairs and sales. 250-537-2853.

Heritage Car and Truck Rentals: At Ganges Marina. Scooter and mountain bike rentals. Free pick-up and drop-off service. 250-537-4225.

Mouat's Store: In Ganges. Cycle supply section in a general store. 250-537-5593.

Salt Spring Kayaking: At the ferry dock in Fulford Harbour. Mountain bike rentals. 250-653-4222.

Salt Spring Marine Rentals: At the head of Ganges Harbour next to Moby's Pub. Bike and scooter rentals. 250-537-9100.

Hang gliding

Off Mount Bruce to designated landing spots in Fulford Valley. Ask for information at the Travel InfoCentre.

Hiking

The degree of difficulty of the trails varies from leisurely strolls down back roads to rigorous hikes through stands of forest and over rocky outcroppings. Only the trails on public land are mentioned in this book. Ask for the Salt Spring Trails and Beach Accesses map at the Tourist InfoCentre. Some examples of the trails are:

Mount Maxwell: Access via Fulford-Ganges Road, Cranberry Road, and Maxwell Road. Spectacular views over Sansum Narrows, Burgoyne Bay, and the Gulf Islands on clear days. Steep, winding drive to the top on a narrow road with frequent washouts. Not recommended for low-slung vehicles or RVs. A number of trails with heavy growth of towering evergreens, salal, and ferns. Rough terrain and unexpected drop-offs at some spots on the trails.

Ruckle Park: At the end of Beaver Point Road at the south end of the island. Undemanding trails with open meadows, rocky beaches, picnic tables, tide pools, outstanding views of passing ferries, glimpses of eagles, and the sounds and smells of the nearby ocean.

Beaver Point Park: On Beaver Point Road just before the entrance to Ruckle Park. Secluded trail begins near the Little Red Schoolhouse, winds through some rare old-growth trees, and then joins the Ruckle Park trails.

Reginald Hill Trails: At the end of Morningside Drive in Fulford Harbour. Vehicles must be left at the gate. Moderately demanding trail with trail markers. Breathtaking views of Fulford Harbour, Burgoyne Valley, and most of the southern Gulf Islands at trail's end.

Peter Arnell Park: On Stewart Road. Access via Fulford-Ganges Road south to Beddis and then Stewart Road. Short, easy trail on the east side of the road with views of Galiano Island and Captain's Passage. Small, tranquil picnic area on the west side of the road.

Mount Erskine: Access from Ganges via Rainbow and then Collins Road. Challenging trail that begins at the end of Collins Road and stops short of the summit at private land.

Mount Bruce: Access by going south on Fulford-Ganges Road and then west on Musgrave Road. Network of good hiking trails in a secluded area. Land ownership changes cause trail changes. Ask at the Travel InfoCentre for information on trails and conditions.

Musgrave Landing: Take Isabella Point Road at the south end of the island west to Musgrave Landing. The road may have washouts and rough spots. Watch for the trail on the left just before the landing and follow it through trees and a meadow to a waterfall and the beach.

Southey Point: Follow Sunset Drive to Southey Point Road at the north end of the island. Watch for trail marker on the right. Short easy walk through the woods brings you to the beach.

Swimming and beach access

Beach accesses are plentiful. It is public land only on the access path itself and below the high water mark. Ask for the Beach Accesses map at the Tourist InfoCentre. Some of the easiest accesses to find and use are:

Beddis Beach: At the end of Beddis Road on the east side of the island. Stone and shell beach at low tide.

Cranberry Outlet: At the end of Collins Road, just south of Booth Bay. A large beach in a bay with easy anchorage, good swimming, and entertaining beachcombing.

Fernwood Government Dock: At junction of Fernwood, Walker Hook, and North Beach roads, near the northeast end of the island.

Quebec Drive: Near the Long Harbour ferry terminal. Small beach with launching spot.

St. Mary Lake: At the north end of St. Mary Lake. Beautiful view down the lake. Easy water entry for children.

Vesuvius Beach: On Bayview Avenue. Approach along Vesuvius Bay Road and watch for the highways department beach access sign. Large, sandy beach at low tide, with warm water and a view stretching down Stuart Channel.

Portlock Park: At the junction of Upper Ganges and Vesuvius Bay roads has a public swimming pool.

Kayaking and canoeing

Island Escapades Adventures: Kayaking and sailing. Two- to six-hour day trips. Two- and three-day packages include bed and breakfast. Beach picnics, hiking, kayaking, and sailing in the southern Gulf Islands. Sunset excursions. Certified wilderness instructor does interpretive hikes. Instruction clinic for kayaking. Climbing gym programs and instruction. Wilderness adventure camps for youth in July and August. 250-537-2537 or 1-888-KAYAK-67.

Salt Spring Kayaking: At the ferry dock in Fulford Harbour. Daily, multi-day, sunset, full-moon, full-provision guided tours of the Gulf Islands. Custom tours available. Instruction. Also bare boat rentals. Kayak sales. 250-653-4222.

Vesuvius Bay.

Salt Spring Marina: Kayaks, rowboats, and canoes. 1-800-334-6629 (in Canada and Washington State) or 250-537-5810.

Salt Spring Marine Rentals: Kayak tours and lessons. Full-moon paddling trips. Canoe and kayak rentals. 250-537-9100.
E-mail: sts@saltspring.com
Web site: http://www.saltspring.com/rentals

Sea Otter Kayaking: In Ganges Harbour. Birding, sunset, and full-moon paddling trips. Lessons, guided tours, sales. Kayak and canoe rentals. 250-537-5678.
E-mail: kayaking@saltspring.com
Web site: http://www.islandnet.com/wtaylor/seaotter.html

Diving

Ken's Mobile Marine Service: Lessons and guided dives. 250-537-9449.
E-mail: kensmobile@saltspring.com

Salt Spring Marina: On Ganges Harbour off Upper Ganges Road. Scuba shop. 1-800-334-6629 in North America or 250-537-5810.

Salt Spring Marine Rentals: Diving charters. 250-537-9100.
E-mail: sts@saltspring.com
Web site: http://www.saltspring.com/rentals

Watercraft rentals

Kayak and canoe rentals

Island Escapades Adventures: 250-537-2537.

Salt Spring Kayaking: 250-537-4664 or 250-653-4222.

Salt Spring Marina: 250-537-5810 or 1-800-334-6629.

Salt Spring Marine Rentals: 250-537-9100.

Sea Otter Kayaking: 250-537-5678.

Powerboat rentals

Salt Spring Marina: 250-537-5810 or 1-800-334-6629.

Salt Spring Marine Rentals: 250-537-9100.
E-mail: sts@saltspring.com
Web site: http://www.saltspring.com/rentals

Charters

Herberg Charters: *MV Genesis*. Hourly, daily, and extended cruises. Bring picnic lunch, binoculars, cameras. 250-537-0907.

Island Escapades Adventures: Kayaking and sailing. Two- to six-hour day trips. Two-and three-day packages include bed and breakfast. Beach picnics, hiking, kayaking, and sailing in the southern Gulf Islands. Sunset excursions. Certified wilderness instructor does interpretive hikes. Instruction clinic for kayaking. 250-537-2537.

Salt Spring Island Boat Tours: Explore Salt Spring and other islands aboard the 57-foot power catamaran *Swan Spirit*. Regularly scheduled 3-hour tours. Individual tickets available. Live commentary about the wildlife, history, ecology, and geology of the area. Sunset cruise with music. Licensed bar. Departs from Ganges Marina. 250-537-0682.
E-mail: boattours@saltspring.com
Web site: http://www.saltspring.com/boattours

Salt Spring Marina: Outfitted power boats, kayaks, rowboats, and canoes. Fishing charters. 1-800-334-6629 or 250-537-5810.

Salt Spring Marine Rentals: Sailing and diving charters, salmon fishing, nature cruises. 250-537-9100.
E-mail: sts@saltspring.com
Web site: http://www.saltspring.com/rentals

Sea Capers Charters: Day tours and half-day tours. 250-537-1150.

Something Fishy: Fishing and sightseeing charters. 250-537-9100 or 250-361-5073.

Picnic spots

Centennial Park: In the centre of Ganges. Picnic tables, swings, and a large grassy area.

Drummond Park: On Fulford Harbour at the south end. Site of a petroglyph—have a look under the trees and into history. Swans gather in this area and are a special addition to this small roadside park.

Long Harbour ferry terminal: Tables on a hill near the terminal—refreshing place to relax and look out over the harbour while waiting for ferry boarding time.

Mount Maxwell Park: Access via Fulford-Ganges Road, Cranberry Road, and Maxwell Road. Tables at a spectacular viewpoint—well worth the long drive up. Road is not suitable for large or low vehicles.

Peter Arnell Park: On Stewart Road. Access via Beddis Road south from Ganges. Picnic tables in a small, secluded park.

Portlock Park: At the junction of Upper and Lower Ganges roads. Picnic tables, public washrooms, playground for children, public tennis courts, and swimming pool.

Ruckle Provincial Park: At the south end of the island. Picnic tables dotted along a rocky shoreline, great views of passing ferries.

Bowling

Kings Lane Recreation: 154 Kings Lane off Lower Ganges Road. Pool tables, billiards, video arcade. 250-537-2054.

Golf

Blackburn Meadows Golf Course: 269 Blackburn Road. Nine-hole 1500-yard course. Open all year. Clubs and pull carts for rent. 250-537-1707. Fax: 250-537-1786.

Salt Spring Golf and Country Club: 805 Lower Ganges Road. At the junction of Upper and Lower Ganges roads. Rolling, rural setting on what was originally a farm. Nine-hole 3147-yard course, rated at 69. Restaurant. Browsing deer and visiting Canada geese add a special dimension to this inviting setting. 250-537-2121.

Tennis

Public courts: At Portlock Park at junction of Upper and Lower Ganges roads and in Fulford on the Fulford Ganges Road near the firehall. 250-537-4448.

Rental courts: At Fulford Marina. 250-653-4467.

Horseback riding

Salt Spring Guided Rides: Year-round scenic guided trail rides through forest and farmland. 250-537-5761.

Places to visit and things to see

Galleries

Salt Spring is unique in Canada for its large number of galleries, studios, and home workshops and for the high quality of the items produced. The number of galleries on the island is increasing, and the quality of work is outstanding. Some galleries are open year round and some only part time. A comprehensive list is available each year from the Tourist InfoCentre. The following is just to give you a taste—ask for a complete listing at the InfoCentre.

Artcraft: In Mahon Hall in Ganges. Main showcase for over two hundred Salt Spring artisans. Summer-long exhibition of high-quality weaving, pottery, jewelry, and many other handcrafted items. Artisans take turns staffing the exhibition. From June to September.

Ewart Gallery: 175 Salt Spring Way. Prestigious shopping for local artists' paintings and sculpture. 250-537-2313.

Jill Louise Campbell Art Gallery: Dockside at the Mouat Centre in Ganges. Art gallery and studio. Watercolour originals, limited edition prints, and cards by resident artist. 250-537-1589. Fax: 250-537-9766.

Naikai Gallery: In Grace Point Square in Ganges. Paintings, pottery, sculpture, jewelry, and gemstones from around the world. Works by international and local artists. 250-537-4400.

Off The Waterfront Gallery: In the Ganges post office building. Handcrafted items by artisans working with silk, sheepskin, wood, metals, pottery, and other materials. 250-537-4525.

Pegasus Gallery: In Mouat's Mall in Ganges. Paintings and prints (some by internationally known wildlife artist Robert Bateman), handcrafted jewelry, and sculpture. Drums, masks, carvings. Emphasis on Native painters and sculptors. Especially arresting display of Northwest Coast Native art. 250-537-2421.

Salt Spring Gems and Art Gallery: In Grace Point Square in Ganges. Precious gems, gold and silver jewelry, paintings. 250-537-4222.

Sophisticated Cow on Hereford: 133 Hereford Avenue. Collection of arts and crafts from over a hundred island artisans. 250-537-0070.

The "Res" Gallery: 221 Langs Road (near the Long Harbour ferry terminal). Features Northwest Coast Native Art. Owner, Fah Ambers, is a Kwakwaka'wakw artist. Specializes in traditional carvings, masks, poles, jewelry, serigraphs, and custom works. By appointment only. 250-537-0753 or 250-537-2868.
E-mail: fah-suki@saltspring.com
Web site: http://www.islandnet.com/saltspring/
Cyber gallery: http://www.islandnet.com/saltspring/island-arts/the-res/the-res.htm

The Stone Fish Studio: At the base of the large hill on the road leading south from

;anges. Focuses on stone sculpture. Some watercolour, wood, and clay items. 250-37-1322.

'he Stone Walrus Gallery: 122 Lower Ganges Road (across from the Tourist InfoCentre). 'rimitive Art gallery with animal motif works from diverse international origins ncluding Haiti, China, Africa, Southwest America (Zuni, Hopi, and Santa Fe). :ollection of carved gemstone animals from Kenya and Peru. Large selection of oloured stone jewelry. 250-537-9896.

'he Tufted Puffin: 340 Scott Point Drive (watch for the sign), off the road to Long Iarbour ferry terminal. Decoys and fine art bird carvings by owner David Jackson whose work is in private collections of Harry Belafonte, Glenn Close, and Prince 'hillip), local and West Coast carvers', potters', and artists' works: soapstone and vood carvings, pottery, burl bowls, raku. 250-537-9939.

'hunderbird Gallery: In Grace Point Square in Ganges. Local and Native artists.)riginal paintings, wood and stone carvings, masks, jewelry. 250-537-1144.

/ortex Gallery: Grace Point Square in Ganges. Contemporary art gallery with sculp- ure, painting, and pottery. 250-537-4749.

\kerman Museum.

)ther special spots

\kerman Museum: 2501 Fulford-Ganges Road. Built in 1993 in honour of the)wner's grandmother, who was the daughter of a Cowichan chief. Native artifacts,)hotographs, and early history. Collection of driftwood. Call ahead or knock on the loor. 250-653-4228.

Chickadee Pine: 217 Baker Road. Handcrafted country-style pine furniture, acces sories, and collectibles made by a husband-and-wife team. Reproductions of 18th and 19th-century works. 250-537-9606.

Chimes and Times: 105 McLennan Drive. Handcrafted cedar wind chimes individu ally tuned. 250-653-2017.

Crossroads: 131 McPhillips in Ganges. Third World store with baskets, crafts, cloth ing, accessories, linens, quilts. 250-537-2122.

Everlasting Summer: 194 McLennan Drive (off Fulford-Ganges Road near Ruckl Park). Three-storey barn filled with flowers hung to dry. Bouquets, wreaths, arrange ments. Formal herb and rose gardens in old English style with hundreds of herbs an a rose arbor. Pottery, candles, oils, seeds, herbal vinegars, and jellies. Classes. Tour by appointment. 250-653-9418.

Illtyd Perkins Woodworking: 1520 Fulford-Ganges Road. Furniture maker and designe Showroom and workshop open by appointment. 250-653-9392.

Meg Buckley Pottery: 2200 Fulford-Ganges Road. Home studio of a potte Functional stoneware and porcelain works. 250-653-4391.

Rose Hill Craft Cottage: 1325 Sunset Drive. Craft cottage on working sheep farm Victorian candle shop and local crafts. Sheepskin rugs. Wool for spinning and fo sweaters and comforters. Farm gate sales of boxed island lamb. Open Sundays an when the sign says Open. 250-537-2082.

Salt Spring Soap Works: In the basement of Mouat's Mall in the centre of Ganges Twenty-year-old family-owned business making handmade vegetable soaps and nat ural body care products. Also produces essential oils and aromatherapy products. On of the owners is a certified aromatherapist. 250-537-2701.

Tom Graham Pottery: Workshop and sales in Fulford next to the ferry terminal Pottery ovenware, dinnerware, and other pieces. 250-653-9593.

The Farm Stand at Indigo Farms: 289 Rainbow Road. Wide range of fruit, vegetables and flowers in season. All locally grown without pesticides. 250-537-5472.

There are many home studios on the island with a wide array of products—weaving pottery, sculpture, jewelry, soap, lotions, flowers, furniture. The studios have varyin hours and open seasons. Ask for the studio map at the Tourist InfoCentre and watc for roadside signs as you move around the island.

Historical sites

Beaver Point School: In Beaver Point Park at the south tip of the island. For many years a one-room schoolhouse, now a small pre-school tucked into the trees an evocative of earlier times.

Viewpoints

Mount Maxwell: Access via Fulford-Ganges Road, Cranberry Road, and Maxwell

Road. On a clear day, there is a breathtaking vista from the top of Mount Maxwell—Sansum Narrows to the west, the San Juan Islands to the south, and the patchwork of Fulford Valley. Burgoyne Bay lies directly below the rock face where the mountain plummets to the ocean. The steep road to the top is not suitable for RVs or low vehicles, and the view is not as far reaching on overcast days.

Guided tours

Island Escapades Adventures: Kayaking and sailing. Two- to six-hour day trips. Two-and three-day packages include bed and breakfast. Beach picnics, hiking, kayaking, and sailing in the southern Gulf Islands. Sunset excursions. Certified wilderness instructor does interpretive hikes. Instruction clinic for kayaking. 250-537-2537.

Salt Spring Kayaking: Daily, multi-day, sunset, full-moon, full-provision guided tours of the Gulf Islands. Custom tours available. 250-653-4222.

Sea Otter Kayaking: Located in Ganges Harbour. Birding, sunset, and full-moon paddles. Lessons and guided tours. 250-537-5678.

Services

All are in Ganges unless otherwise stated. Mouat's Mall and Grace Point Square are in the centre of Ganges at the waterfront on Ganges Harbour. Creekside is on McPhillips Avenue. Gasoline Alley is beside Centennial Park in the centre of Ganges. The Upper Ganges Centre is on Upper Ganges Road going toward Vesuvius.

Bakeries
Barb's Buns 250-537-4491
Embe Bakery 250-537-5611
Sweet Arts 250-537-4205
Thrifty Foods 250-537-1522

Banks
Bank of Montreal 250-537-5524
Canadian Imperial Bank of Commerce 250-537-5584
Island Savings Credit Union 250-537-5587

Bookstores
Brook's Books and Tunes in lower Mouat's Mall 250-537-9874
Et cetera on Hereford Avenue 250-537-5115
Island Books Plus on McPhillips Avenue 250-537-2812
Parkside News beside Centennial Park 250-537-2861
Volume II in Mouat's Mall 250-537-9223

Car rentals
Ganges Marina on the Lower Ganges Road 250-537-5242
Heritage Car and Truck Rentals 250-537-4225

Rainbow Rentals—car and truck rentals 250-537-2877
Salt Spring Marine Rentals—scooter rentals 250-537-9100

Car wash
Island Car Wash at 270 Park Drive 250-537-4717

Churches and religions
Anglican Church 250-537-2171
Baha'i Faith 250-537-9871 or 250-537-5188
Baptist Church 250-537-2222
Buddhist 250-537-2378 or 250-380-8610
Church of Jesus Christ of Latter Day Saints 250-653-4430
Full Gospel Chapel 250-537-2622
Eckankar Societies of Canada 250-653-4034
Jehovah's Witnesses 250-537-9726
Our Lady of Grace 250-537-2150
Pentecostal Assembly 250-537-4143
Roman Catholic Church 250-537-2150
United Church 250-537-5812

Cycle rental and repair
Bicycle Bob's 250-537-2853
Salt Spring Marine Rentals 250-537-9100

Drugstore
Pharmasave 250-537-5534

Fax service
Et cetera at 120 Hereford Avenue 250-537-5115
Sargeant's Mercantile in Fulford 250-653-9600

Fishing supplies and licenses
Mouat's Store 250-537-5593
Fulford Marina (supplies only) 250-653-4467
Ganges Marina 250-537-5242
Post Office in Fulford (licenses only) 250-653-4313
Harbours End Marina 250-537-4202
Salt Spring Marine Rentals 250-537-9100

Grocery stores
Creekside Seafood, Poultry, and Sushi 250-537-5088
Fat Rascal Meat and Deli 250-537-5236
Mobile Market 250-537-1784
The Farmstand at Indigo Farms 250-537-5472
The Fishery 250-537-2457
Thrifty Foods 250-537-1522
Ganges Village Market 250-537-4144
Harbour Food Market 250-537-2460
NatureWorks Natural Foods 250-537-2325

Vesuvius Store on Vesuvius Bay Road near the ferry terminal 250-537-1515
Sargeant's Mercantile at Fernwood Road and Walker Hook Road 250-537-2451
Patterson's Store in Fulford 250-653-4321
Sargeant's Mercantile at Fulford Marina 250-653-9600

Trilliums.

Hospital
Lady Minto Hospital on Crofton Road off Lower Ganges Road 250-250-537-5545
Fax: 250-537-1475

Launching sites
see map on pages 52-55

Laundromats
Mrs. Clean Laundromat & Showers in Gasoline Alley 250-537-4133
New Wave Laundry Services at 126 Upper Ganges Road 250-537-2500
Salt Spring Marina 250-537-5810
Ganges Marina 250-537-5242

Library
On McPhillips Avenue 250-537-4666

Liquor store
In Grace Point Centre 250-537-5441

Marine charts
Et cetera at 120 Hereford Avenue 250-537-5115
Volume II in Mouat's Mall 250-537-9223

Marine repair
Ken's Mobile Marine Service 250-537-9449

Harbours End Marina 250-537-4202

Pay telephones
All B.C. Ferry terminals
Government wharf at Centennial Park
Trading Company grocery store
Ganges Village Market
The Salty Shop
Salt Spring Marina
Harbour House Hotel
Portlock Park
Fulford Marina
Fulford post office
Fulford Inn
Ruckle Park
At most resorts

Pharmacy
Pharmasave 250-537-5534

Photofinishing
Apple Photo on Hereford Avenue across from the Tourist InfoCentre 250-537-9917
Color King at Grace Point Square (1-hour service) 250-537-2131
Sargeant's Mercantile in Fulford 250-653-9600

Post offices
Ganges 250-537-2321
Harbour Food Market 250-537-2460
Fulford 250-653-4313

Propane
Ganges Marina 250-537-5242
Salt Spring Marina 250-537-5810 or 1-800-334-6629

Public transportation
Salt Spring Taxi 250-537-9712
Salt Spring Bus Company/Limousine/Taxi 250-537-4737 or 1-888-537-4737
Gulf Island Water Taxi 250-537-2510
Inter Island Launch Water Taxi 250-656-8788

Public washrooms
Centennial Park in Ganges
Long Harbour and Fulford ferry terminals

RCMP
250-537-5555

Recreation centre
154 Kings Lane (bowling, pool, video arcade) 250-537-2054

Deer on Salt Spring Island.

Showers
Mrs. Clean Laundromat in Ganges at Gasoline Alley 250-537-4133
Fulford Marina at Fulford Harbour 250-653-9600
Salt Spring Marina 250-537-5810

Swimming pool
At Portlock Park at the junction of Upper and Lower Ganges roads 250-537-4448

Tennis
At Portlock Park 250-537-4448
At Fulford Marina 250-653-9600

Theatre
Cinema Central in Central Hall at junction of Vesuvius Bay and Upper Ganges roads (blackboard outside lists titles, times, and dates) 250-537-4656

Travel InfoCentre
In Ganges near the firehall
P.O. Box 111
Ganges, BC V0S 1E0
250-537-5252 Fax: 250-537-4276
E-mail: chamber@saltspring.com
Web site: http://www.saltspringisland.bc.ca

Access by boat

Government docks

Ganges docks: At Mouat's Mall, at Centennial Park, and in Ganges Harbour near the

Harbour House Hotel.

Fernwood Dock: At Fernwood Road on the northeast end of the island. Short walk to small grocery store, gas pumps, pay phone.

Fulford Dock: Near the Fulford ferry terminal (south end of the island). Near Fulford Marina, where there are fuel and water, marine supplies and repairs, showers and toilets, deli diner, grocery store, in-house bakery. Short walk to Fulford Harbour's post office, restaurants, gas station, artisans' galleries.

Vesuvius Dock: At the ferry dock on the northwest side of the island. Short walk to public beach, Vesuvius Pub, Seaside Kitchen family restaurant, Beachcomber Motel, Vesuvius corner store, pay phone.

Burgoyne Bay: On the west side of the island. Isolated area where log booming is done. Far from stores and facilities.

Musgrave Landing: Very isolated area on the south end of the island, far from facilities.

Marinas

Fulford Harbour Marina: In Fulford Harbour. All season overnight moorage with reservations accepted. Fuel, power and water, boaters' supplies and hardware. Boat repairs nearby. Sargeant's Mercantile grocery store with deli diner, fax and courier services, pay phone. Public washrooms and showers. Picnic tables, tennis court, play area. Fishing supplies (no licenses). 250-653-4467. Fax: 250-653-4457. VHF 68. E-mail: fulfordmarina@saltspring.com
Web site: http://www.saltspring.com/fulfordmarina

Ganges Marina: In Ganges Harbour. Moorage, gas and diesel fuel, propane, fishing gear, bait, and licenses. Car, truck, and scooter rentals. Shower and laundry. Short walk to facilities and shopping. 250-537-5242.

Harbours End Marina: In Ganges Harbour. Marine parts, service, and repairs. Tackle, bait, and fishing licenses. Short walk to facilities and shopping. 250-537-4202.

Salt Spring Marina: In Ganges Harbour. Guest moorage. Marine sales and service. Showers, laundromat. Provisions and beer. Bait and tackle. Pay phone. Propane. Bed and breakfast accommodation. Scuba supplies and air. Power and water on docks. Home of Moby's Marine Pub with great food until midnight, entertainment and dancing. Fishing charters. Boat, kayak, and scooter rentals. 250-537-5810 or 1-800-334-6629 (in Canada and Washington State).

Loop Routes

These routes will lead you to some intriguing spots whether you travel by car or bicycle. Watch for roadside signs along the way for galleries and home studios—new ones are opening all the time.

Route 1: Beginning from Long Harbour

Turn left at the first stop sign. Ganges, just around several curves, is the largest town on the island and an eclectic mix of old and new clustered around three indentations in the harbour.

As you arrive in town, watch for Artcraft (in summer) in the Mahon Hall, on your right. This large exhibition of high-quality weaving, pottery, jewelry, and many other handcrafted items—island artistry at its best—runs from June through the Labour Day weekend (the first weekend in September). Artisans compete for admission of their products and take turns staffing the exhibition. This is an outstanding show and a not-to-be-missed item for your agenda.

Next, stop at the Travel InfoCentre on your left. Friendly locals will make every effort to supply you with information.

Ganges Harbour and Mouat's Mall.

Stroll down Hereford Avenue to Et cetera bookstore with its wide selection of local interest books, marine charts, and general reading materials.

Then visit the Sophisticated Cow at 133 Hereford Avenue. There, in a heritage house framed by gardens, you will find a collection of arts and crafts from over a hundred island artists.

Go back past the InfoCentre and to the post office building where you will find the Off the Waterfront Gallery, a co-op owned and operated by local artisans. Browse among handmade items of silk, wool, wood, pottery, and more.

Cross the street to the large green and white building, Mouat's General Store, a feature of island life for many years. In the halls are authentic records of life as it used to be on Salt Spring—old photos of settlers, machinery, buildings, and special events.

Go downstairs to Salt Spring Soap Works, a twenty-year-old family business producing vegetable based soaps and natural body care products.

Browse in Volume II Book Store on the dock side of Mouat's store. This cozy, well-stocked shop has an aged wood interior and windows overlooking the water. The wide selection of bestsellers, classics, and general reading includes a particularly good representation of local and British Columbia writers' works.

In the same building, browse through Pegasus Gallery where the emphasis is on Native and West Coast works. The high calibre paintings and prints (some by internationally known wildlife artist Robert Bateman), handcrafted jewelry, and sculpture form an arresting display.

Stroll along to Centennial Park—relax on the grass and walk the waterside boardwalk and the docks where commercial fishing boats, pleasure craft, and sailboats are moored. Savour the feeling created by the mix of boats docked there and then sit on the captain's bench near the rock cairn and fountain.

Ready for other treats? Head for Harlan's Chocolate Treats across the street. Harlan creates delectable, prize-winning liqueur truffles and buttery fudges. You will find fresh-roasted coffees, specialty teas, gourmet ice cream, and frozen yogurt there too. Another choice is to follow the street to Embe Bakery at the bottom of the hill. They have a wide array of fresh-baked breads and sweets and the coffee pot is always on. Enjoy the treat of your choice at the tables outside.

Route 2: Beginning at Ganges

Go south from Ganges on Fulford-Ganges Road, through the beautiful Hundred Hills area just outside Ganges. The long entrance to Ganges harbour lies on your left with the surrounding islands forming layers of backdrop. On clear days, Mount Baker towers majestically over the scene. Sailboats glide in and out and, in the distance, ferries work their way through the islands.

Follow Cranberry Road (on the right) 9 kilometres to the top of Mount Maxwell for a stupendous view of surrounding countryside, islands, and ocean. However, the road is not suitable for RVs or low vehicles.

Return to Fulford-Ganges Road and wind south toward Fulford Harbour. Stop at Meg Buckley's pottery studio at 2200 Fulford-Ganges Road where she produces both stoneware and porcelain.

Stop in at the Bob Akerman Museum at 2501 Fulford-Ganges Road, a log building on your left. Bob Akerman lives in the house beside the museum—just knock on the door. Browse in the past among many staples of Native life, a driftwood collection, and old photographs. Chat with Bob about the history of Salt Spring and its peoples.

Note St. Paul's Roman Catholic Church at the head of Fulford Harbour. The stones and supplies for its construction were transported from Vancouver Island by canoe and then by oxen and stoneboat in the 1880s.

Take some time to watch the swans that gather in the harbour in front of Fulford Inn and look for the petroglyph hidden under the trees at Drummond Park on Isabella Point Road.

If you are looking for really special accommodation, check in at the oceanfront retreat for two beside the marina—a real windmill.

Ganges Harbour - Hundred Hills area.

Drop in at Sargeant's Mercantile store in the Fulford Marina building. This is a multi-purpose store with a difference—there is a "made in British Columbia" section and other items can be ordered through their catalogue. There is a deli diner here, too, with an in-store bakery and gourmet pizzas. Sit at the outdoor tables or use the gazebo and play areas.

Visit Ruckle Park on the south tip of the island. This route takes you through heavily wooded farmland where sheep browse in the fields and roadside stands have honour boxes for vegetables and flowers.

Watch for McLennan Drive and drop in at Everlasting Summer Dried Flower Farm at 194 McLennan Drive. Stroll through the multi-coloured gardens and along the wooded path. Visit the formal herb and rose garden in old English style with hundreds of herbs and a rose arbor. Surround yourself with fragrance and beauty in the three-storey barn where flowers hang to dry. Choose from their bouquets, wreaths, and arrangements—take home some everlasting summer. Visit the gallery, where local artists' work is displayed. Watch for artist demonstrations on Sundays.

Stroll along the unspoiled seashore in Ruckle Park at the end of the road. Climb on the rocks or just sit and watch the ferries glide by. This park is a real haven with many trails, fascinating shoreline marine life, and bird-watching possibilities.

Return to Fulford Harbour and drop in at Patterson's store, a third-generation general store stocked with everything from clothes to food, books, and small tools. Visit Tom Graham's pottery workshop and showroom in Fulford (near the ferry terminal) where he crafts pottery ovenware, dinnerware, and other pieces.

Finally, fill up on home-cooked soup or pie at Rodrigo's Restaurant while watching the ferry come and go, or drop in at the Salt Spring Roasting Company for coffee, tea, panini, and more.

St. Paul's Church and Fulford Inn.

Route 3: From Ganges to Vesuvius

Leave Ganges following Lower Ganges Road. Stop for coffee or a meal at Dagwood's Diner in the Upper Ganges Mall on your left. Wind through pleasant, treed areas to the junction of Upper and Lower Ganges roads. Turn left at the signs to Vesuvius. Watch for Mark's Pottery on the right. This is the studio and home of Mark Meredith, long-time resident and potter. After returning to the road, turn left at the sign for the public beach access, and go to Vesuvius Beach for a swim or beach walk, depending on the time and tides. Pick up provisions at Vesuvius corner store, near the ferry terminal. Have a snack at the Seaside Kitchen or on the deck at Vesuvius Pub while the ferry sails back and forth across the channel against the backdrop of the mountains on Vancouver Island.

Special events

Visit Salt Spring Sojourn's web site at http://www.islandnet.com/saltspring/ for a comprehensive listing of the many and varied events that take place on Salt Spring each year.

Saturday Morning Market: Every Saturday in Centennial Park. Home-baked goods, handcrafts, flowers and much more. Festive, longstanding feature of Salt Spring.

Polar Bear Swim: In January at Vesuvius Bay.

Trout Derby: In February at Cedar Beach Resort.

Around the Island Sailing Race: Annual sailboat race in May.

Artcraft: From June through Labour Day (the first weekend in September). In Mahon Hall in the centre of Ganges. Over two hundred artisans' weaving, silver and costume jewelry, woodwork, quilting, and many other items.

Sea Capers: In mid-June. In Ganges. Celebration of Captain Cook's arrival in this area over two hundred years ago. Infectious celebration over three days, with a pancake breakfast, parade, games, and competitions for all ages. Lots of food, beef and salmon barbecue, beer garden, live music, challenging water sports events, and a sand castle contest for all ages.

Everlasting Summer Annual Garden Faire and Music Festival: In July. At Everlasting Summer Dried Flower and Herb Farm at 194 McLennan Road on the south end of the island. Art, handcrafts, food, artisans' works, plus Folk, Celtic, and Bluegrass music in the Herb and Rose garden. 250-653-9418.

Wine Festival: By the Tuned Air Choir. Early July at the Farmers' Institute grounds on Rainbow Road. Wine merchants, wine tasting, pianist, choral music. Shuttle bus provided for boaters.

Festival of the Arts: In July. At various locations in Ganges. Music, theatre, dance, poetry, comedy, family entertainment.

Jazz Festival: In July. In Ganges. Full jazz program with bands from many areas of B.C.

Fall Fair: Saturday in mid-September. At the Fair Grounds on Rainbow Road. Prize-winning vegetables, animals, and baked goods. Good, old-fashioned fun with sheep dog trials, apple juice pressed on the spot, and a beef and lamb barbecue.

Ferry at Beaver Point at Ruckle Park.

Guild Christmas Show and Sale: In November in Mahon Hall in Ganges. Products from the many artisans on the island: pottery, paintings, jewelry, weaving, woodwork.

Beaver Point Hall Christmas Craft Fair: In December. At Beaver Point Hall on the south end, near Beaver Point Park. Knitting, weaving, homemade jams, and many delightful, handmade items by island craftspeople.

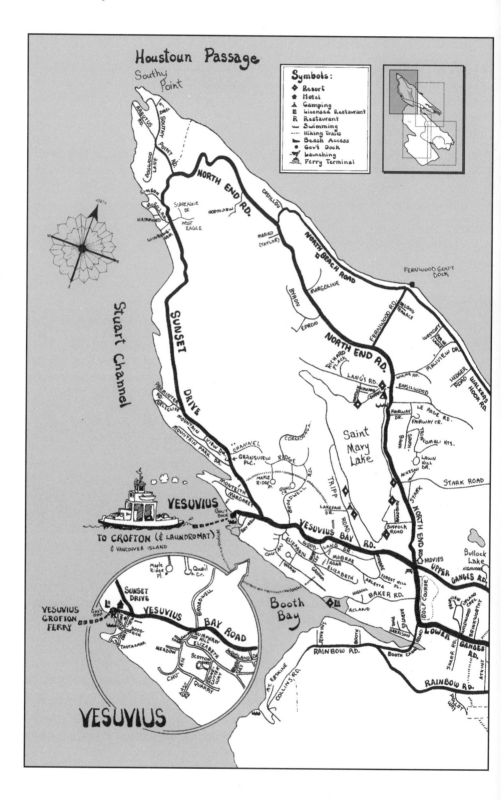

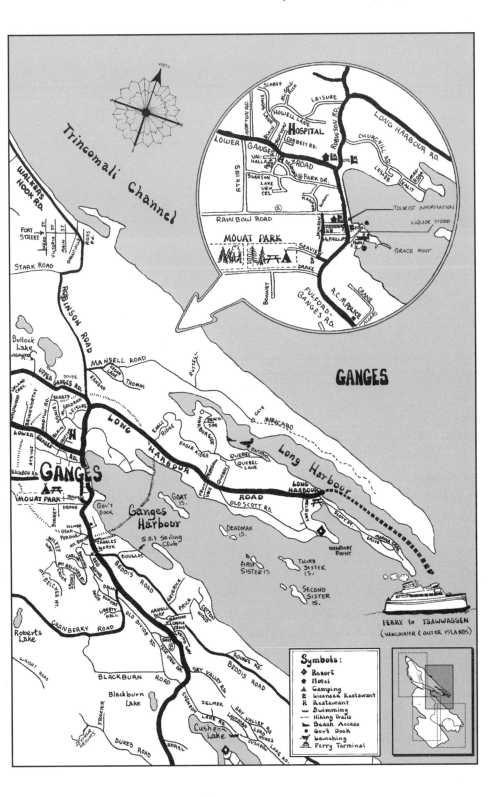

Symbols:
◆ Resort
⚑ Motel
▲ Camping
Ɛ Licensed Restaurant
R Restaurant
≈ Swimming
---- Hiking Trails
⊨ Beach Access
● Gov't Dock
⚓ Launching
⛴ Ferry Terminal

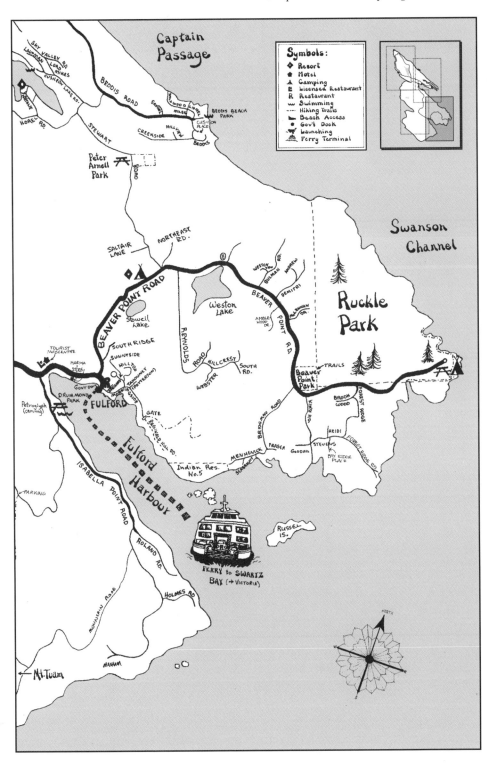

Chapter Two

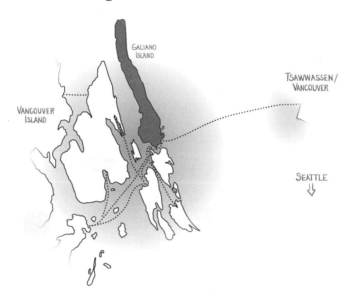

Galiano Island

island with easiest access from mainland B.C. • tranquillity • rustic charm • quiet country atmosphere • seascape views • hiking • cycling • kayaking and canoeing • ocean swimming • beachcombing • picnic spots • boat charters • scuba diving • golfing • horseback riding • government docks • marina • galleries • artists' and artisans' home studios • summer fair • blackberry festival • weavers' and spinners' sale • resorts • lodges • inns • bed and breakfasts • campgrounds • restaurants • pubs • pub bus for boaters

Galiano Island lies between the British Columbia mainland and Vancouver Island like a boundary between the bustle of the city and the serenity of the Gulf Islands. The population is about a thousand. Little commercial or residential development has taken place on this densely wooded island. Magnificent Douglas fir trees over three hundred years old are still standing. The coastline provides marine and mountain views with many opportunities for exploring by land and by sea. Rainfall averages about 30 centimetres (25 inches) per year and prickly pear cactus grow along the south shore.

Getting to Galiano by ferry

Getting to Galiano Island from the B.C. mainland by B.C. Ferries

1. From Tsawwassen to Sturdies Bay on Galiano Island: This is the most direct route from the mainland to Galiano Island. Tsawwassen is 37 kilometres (about forty minutes) southwest of Vancouver on Highway 17. Sailing time is about fifty minutes. Reservations taken. Food service.

2. From Tsawwassen to Swartz Bay on Vancouver Island and from Swartz Bay to Sturdies Bay on Galiano Island: Sailing time from Tsawwassen to Swartz Bay is about an hour and a half. Sailing time from Swartz Bay to Galiano Island varies depending on the number of stops. Check the schedule for details. Ask the cashier for a transfer at Tsawwassen. No reservations taken. Food service on the Tsawwassen to Swartz Bay route.

Sandstone sculpture, Montague Harbour, Galiano Island.

3. From Horseshoe Bay to Departure Bay (Nanaimo) on Vancouver Island, from Departure Bay to Swartz Bay, and from Swartz Bay to Sturdies Bay on Galiano Island: Horseshoe Bay is 23 kilometres (about thirty-five minutes) north of Vancouver. Sailing time from Horseshoe Bay to Departure Bay is about an hour and a half. From Nanaimo drive 132 kilometres (about two and a half hours) south to Swartz Bay and take the ferry to Sturdies Bay on Galiano Island. Sailing times vary depending on the number of stops. Check the schedule for details. No reservations taken. Food service.

Getting to Galiano from Vancouver Island by B.C. Ferries

From Swartz Bay to Sturdies Bay on Galiano Island: Swartz Bay is on Vancouver Island, 30 kilometres (forty-five minutes) north of Victoria. Sailing times vary depending on the number of stops. No reservations taken. Food service.

B.C. Ferries schedule information and reservations
British Columbia Ferries
1112 Fort Street
Victoria, BC V8V 4V2
Web site: http://www.bcferries.bc.ca
In British Columbia: 1-888-223-3779
Outside British Columbia: 250-386-3431

Getting to Galiano from the United States
1. From Tsawwassen, B.C. by B.C. Ferries: Drive to Tsawwassen, B.C., 230 kilometres north of Seattle, on Interstate Highway 5 and, in Canada, Highways 99 and 17. Sail directly to Sturdies Bay on Galiano Island or sail from Tsawwassen to Swartz Bay on Vancouver Island (one and a half hours) and then transfer to the ferry going to Sturdies Bay on Galiano Island. Reservations taken and food service on the Tsawwassen to Sturdies Bay route.

B.C. Ferries schedule information and reservations
British Columbia Ferries
1112 Fort Street
Victoria, BC V8V 4V2
Web site: http://www.bcferries.bc.ca
In British Columbia: 1-888-223-3779
Outside British Columbia: 250-386-3431
    B.C. Ferries accepts Visa and MasterCard for reservations and Visa, MasterCard, and Canadian and American currency at check-in. There are ATM machines and a currency exchange at the Tsawwassen terminal.

2. From Anacortes, Washington by Washington State ferry system: Drive to Anacortes (85 miles north and 20 miles west of Seattle) and sail to Sidney, B.C. Sailing time is three hours. Reservations taken. Food service. From Sidney, drive 8 kilometres (fifteen minutes) to the B.C. Ferry terminal at Swartz Bay and catch the ferry to Sturdies Bay on Galiano Island.

Washington State Ferries schedule information and reservations
Washington State Ferries
Pier 52
801 Alaskan Way
Seattle, WA 98104-1487
E-mail: wsf@wsdot.wa.gov
Web site: http://www.wsdot.wa.gov/ferries/
In U.S.: 1-800-843-3779
Outside U.S.: 206-464-6400

3. From Seattle, Washington by the Princess Marguerite (Clipper Navigation): Sail from Seattle to Victoria, B.C. Sailing time is four and a half hours. Reservations taken. Food service. From Victoria, drive 30 kilometres (forty-five minutes) to the B.C. Ferries terminal at Swartz Bay and take the ferry to Sturdies Bay on Galiano Island.

Clipper Navigation schedule information and reservations
Clipper Navigation
2701 Alaskan Way
Pier 69
Seattle, WA 98121
E-mail: clipper@nwlink.com
Web site: http://www.victoriaclipper.com/
In U.S.: 1-800-888-2535
Outside U.S.: 206-448-5000

4. From Port Angeles, Washington (on the Olympic Peninsula) by Black Ball Transport ferry: Drive to Port Angeles and sail on the Black Ball Transport ferry to Victoria, B.C. Sailing time is one and a half hours. No reservations taken. Food service. From Victoria, drive 30 kilometres (forty-five minutes) to the B.C. Ferries terminal at Swartz Bay and take the ferry to Galiano Island.

Black Ball Transport ferry schedule information and reservations
Black Ball Transport
430 Belleville Street
Victoria, BC V8V 1W9
Web site: http://www.northolympic.com/coho
In U.S.: 360-457-4491
In Canada: 250-386-2202

Accommodation

Plan ahead for accommodation because facilities are limited, heavily booked at the height of the tourist season, and often closed in the off-season.

Other resources

Galiano Getaways 250-539-5551

Galiano Island Travel InfoCentre
P.O. Box 73
Galiano Island, BC V0N 1P0
250-539-2233 Fax: 250-539-2233
Web site: http://www.islandnet.com/galiano

Canadian Gulf Islands Reservation Service
637 Southwind Road
Galiano Island, BC V0N 1P0
250-539-5390 Fax: 250-539-5390
E-mail: reservations@gulfislands.com

Race Point Lighthouse, Galiano Island.

Web site: http://www.multimedia.bcit.bc.ca/b&b

British Columbia Bed and Breakfast Association
101—1001 West Broadway
Vancouver, BC V6H 4V1
604-734-3486 Fax: 604-985-6037

Island Escapades Adventures
118 Natalie Lane
Ganges, BC V8K 2C6
250-537-2537 Fax: 250-537-2532

Ministry of Tourism
Travel Reservation and Information Service
In Greater Vancouver: 663-6000
In North America, outside Greater Vancouver: 1-800-663-6000
Outside North America: 250-387-1642
Web site: http://www.tbc.gov.bc.ca/tourism/information.html

Resorts, lodges, inns

There are no restaurants on the premises in the following listings unless mentioned.

Bodega Resort: 120 Monasty Road (corner of Porlier Pass Road and Cook Road near the north end of the island). Quiet retreat in a pastoral setting on 25 acres. Log chalets with fireplaces. Bed and breakfast accommodation in the lodge. Trail rides. Restaurant open in the summer. Accommodation and restaurant facilities available for groups (10 or more) by prior arrangement year round. Meeting room on the premises. 250-539-

2677.

Driftwood Village Resort: 205 Bluff Road East (at south end of the island). Cozy, fully equipped cottages in tranquil setting. Fireplaces, natural wood and rattan furnishings, kitchens, full baths, some with Jacuzzis, decks with ocean views. Beach access nearby. Garden hot tub. Original art in the cottages. Pets welcome. Ferry pick-up. Weekly and off-season rates. 250-539-5457.

Galiano Lodge: 134 Madrona Drive. Seventeen rooms in two separate buildings, all with views of Active Pass and Mount Baker. Oceanfront lodge has wood-burning fireplaces, down comforters, private balconies or garden patios, Jacuzzis, soaker tubs. Beachside guest rooms have private baths and sitting areas. Fully equipped private

Fireweed on Galiano Island.

meeting room. Five-minute walk from the ferry. Ferry pick-up available. Boardroom/conference facilities. 250-539-3388. Fax: 250-539-3338.

La Berengerie: 2806 Montague Harbour Road (at Clanton Road). Secluded country inn with a European feel, about ten minutes' walk from Montague Harbour. Hot tub. Antique furnishings. Gourmet French cuisine. Local art displayed. Ferry pick-up. Bed and breakfast rates. Closed December through February. Reservations recommended. 250-539-5392.

Madrona Lodge: On Porlier Pass Road (northwest end of the island). One-, two-, and three-bedroom log cottages in the forest by the sea. Boat ramp and courtesy moorage, bikes and rowboats. Air compressor for divers. Home of Galiano Island Diving Services. Good diving in the vicinity. Meeting room and dining facilities for registered guests. Off-season rates. 250-539-2926.

Sutil Lodge Heritage Guest House: 637 Southwind Drive in Montague Harbour.

Heritage building built in 1928, sheltered by magnificent maples at the waterfront on twenty secluded, wooded acres. Décor from the 1930s. Sitting room and dining room with fireplaces. Bed and breakfast rates. Accommodates groups. Complimentary canoes. Sea kayak rentals. Badminton. Home of *Great White Cloud* catamaran cruises. 250-539-2930.

The Cliffhouse: Off Ganner Drive (mid-island). Unique, secluded waterfront cottage. Panoramic views. Complimentary bikes and canoe. 250-539-5239.

Woodstone Country Inn: 743 Georgeson Bay Road near Sturdies Bay Road. Tranquil valley or forest view. Close to beach and Montague Harbour Park. Gracious accommodation with fireplaces, antiques, and wicker. Gourmet, licensed dining. Country breakfast and afternoon tea included. All rooms have private baths and most have fireplaces. Adult-oriented. Wheelchair accessible. 250-539-2022.

Bed and breakfasts

Bed and breakfast fliers are available on the free information racks on most British Columbia ferries. Reservations are strongly recommended. The Galiano Island Chamber of Commerce runs an information booth, near the ferry terminal, that provides information on accommodation.

Some bed and breakfasts operating year round are:

Cliff Pagoda: 2851 Montague Harbour Road. Japanese-style house perched on a cliff overlooking the harbour. Spectacular view and sunsets. Hot tub and sauna. Meditation room. Gourmet health food. Lunch and dinner on the premises can be arranged. Complimentary ferry pick-up for cyclists and foot passengers. Canoe and bikes available. 250-539-2260.

Moonshadows: 771 Georgeson Bay Road. Luxurious home with pastoral view. Huge stone fireplace with outdoor hot tub overlooking pond and field. Spacious rooms with ensuite facilities. Gourmet breakfasts. Free ferry pick-up. Adults only. 250-539-5544.

Morning Beach: 109 Harper Road near Sturdies Bay. Tranquil waterfront location. Sandy beach, panoramic view, oceanside deck, hot tub. Fishing and sightseeing available. B&B or self-contained. 250-539-3053 or 604-596-7986.

Mount Galiano Eagle's Nest: 2-720 Active Pass Drive. Artist's home overlooking one kilometre of private oceanfront. Wilderness trails lead to unforgettable vistas of the islands. Ten minutes from the ferry. Complimentary ferry pick-up. 250-539-2567.

Polly's Place: 2416 Sturdies Bay Road. Cozy with choice of breakfasts. Relaxing garden. Low rates. Five-minute walk from ferry. 250-539-2541.

Serenity by the Sea: 225 Serenity Lane. Waterfront panoramas, spectacular home, waterfall garden. Private cabin/chalet. Terraced tub by the ocean. Massage and reiki available. Custom retreats. 250-539-2655 or 1-800-944-2655.

Tide Winds: 214 Gulf Road. Lowbank oceanfront home. Five-minute walk from the ferry. Panoramic view of Strait of Georgia, Active Pass, and Mount Baker. Heart breakfasts. Accommodations include large ensuite bedroom with private balcony, fire place, queen-sized bed. 250-539-2478.

Campgrounds

Montague Harbour Provincial Marine Park: The only public camping facility. Twenty five drive-in and fifteen walk-in sites, some reservable. One reservable group site for forty people. Nature programs on request. Idyllic setting on a bay with sandy beach for swimming. 1-800-689-9025.

Restaurants, pubs, and take-out food

Bodega Resort: 120 Monasty Road at Porlier Pass and Cook roads. Summer only. 250 539-2677.

Daystar Market Café: 96 Georgeson Bay Road (at the junction of Sturdies Bay and Georgeson Bay roads). Specialty dining with regular and vegetarian menus. Accent c health foods and organics. Espresso bar. Indoor and outdoor dining. Lunch and dinner served during summer. Display of local artists' works. Reservations accepted Licensed. 250-539-2800.

Galiano Lodge: 134 Madrona Drive. Fine dining at the oceanfront. West Coast cuisin Reservations strongly recommended. Display of local artists' works. Very close to the ferry. Licensed. 250-539-3388.

Hummingbird Pub: At junction of Sturdies Bay and Georgeson Bay road Neighbourhood pub with cozy interior, fireplace, and scrumptious food from burge to gourmet. Seafood a specialty in season. Take-out food and picnic area. Live ente tainment on weekends. No minors in the pub. Family picnic tables outside. Pub bu runs between Montague Harbour Park gate, the Montague Marina junction, and the pub as a service to campers and boaters from the May long weekend to the end of September. Licensed. 250-539-5472.

La Berengerie: 2806 Montague Harbour Road (at Clanton Road). About ten minute walk from Montague Harbour or a few minutes' drive from the ferry terminal. Frenc cuisine in a secluded setting. Closed December through February. Reservations rec ommended. Licensed. 250-539-5392.

Max and Moritz Spicy Island Food House: At the ferry terminal. German and Inde nesian food. Outside seating. Home delivery within 10 kilometres. 250-539-5888.

Montague Marina Coffee Bar: Cappuccino, baked goods, breakfasts, bagels, lunche Inside and deck tables. Licensed. 250-539-5733.

The Tee House: On St. Andrews Road just off Ellis and Linklater roads. Lounge and resta rant at the Galiano Golf and Country Club. Open to the public. Licensed. 250-539-5533

Woodstone Country Inn.

Trincomali Bakery and Deli: On Sturdies Bay Road near the ferry terminal. Pizza, espresso, bakery items. Breakfast, lunch, and dinner. Inside and outside seating. 250-539-2004.

Woodstone Country Inn: 734 Georgeson Bay Road. Fine dining in a pastoral setting overlooking farm fields. Emphasis on local seafood and meats, organically grown vegetables and herbs. Reservations recommended. Licensed. 250-539-2022.

Take-out food

Max and Moritz Spicy Island Food House: At the ferry terminal. German and Indonesian food. Home delivery within 10 kilometres. 250-539-5888.

Scoopy Doos: On Sturdies Bay Road near the ferry terminal. Ice cream, sundaes, floats, milkshakes, yogurt, juice bar, take-home desserts. 250-539-2388.

Trincomali Bakery and Deli: On Sturdies Bay Road at the Deli Mall. European-style pastries, home-style bread and buns. Pizza. Full service deli. All natural products. Specialty coffees and teas, cappuccino. Near the ferry terminal. 250-539-2004.

Activities

Cycling

Cycling is a pleasure here. The roads have long, straight stretches as well as some winding sections. They lead through the heavily treed landscape, yet are never far from the sound, sight, and smell of the ocean. Many of the roads are paved and the shoulder width varies. See the Loop Route section for a suggested route.

Cycling supplies, rentals, repairs

Ben's Bikes: Mountain bike rentals. 250-539-2442.

Galiano Bicycle Rental and Repairs: 36 Burrill Road (off Bluff Road). Twenty-one-gear mountain bike rentals (with racks and helmets) and repairs. Tandems and child trailers. Accessory shop. After-hours repair service. Bike delivery. Matthew Schoenfeld and Pam Taylor. 250-539-9906.

Hiking

There are many excellent, scenic trails with varying degrees of difficulty. Only the trails on public land are described here. You can hike along the eastern side of the island or on the ridges, which have spectacular views of Vancouver Island. These trails are on private land but have been used by the public for years. Ask about access at the Travel InfoCentre near the ferry.

Bellhouse Park: At the end of Jack Drive near the ferry terminal. A short, captivating walk at the ocean's edge. Passing ferries, a lightstation across the pass, bald eagles, rocky shorelines.

Dionisio Point, Galiano Island.

Bluffs Park: Over three hundred acres with many trails and beachfront on Active Pass. Numerous viewpoints—an especially spellbinding one overlooking Georgeson Bay. Access from the ferry via either by Burrill and Bluff roads or by following Sturdies Bay Road to Georgeson Bay Road and turning right onto Bluff Road.

Dionisio Point Provincial Park: At the north end of Galiano at Coon Bay. Accessible by water only.

Montague Harbour Provincial Park: Near the government dock at Montague Harbour. An idyllic, natural harbour. Many public trails. Ask for information at the Travel InfoCentre.

Swimming and beach access

Montague, Bellhouse, and Bluffs parks have public beaches. The beach at Sturdies Bay is easily reached on foot from the ferry terminal. Retreat Cove (about half way to the north end of the island) has a pleasant beach and swimming area.

The water is warmer on the east side of the island than on the west side. You can beachcomb below the high water mark along the whole east side of the island when the tide is out.

Kayaking and canoeing

Ben's Gulf Island Kayaking: Guided canoe and kayak trips. Day, sunset, camping, and B&B tours. Canoe and kayak rentals. Naturalist tours. No experience required. 250-539-2442.

Galiano Island Sea Kayaking: 637 Southwind Drive. Guided tours in the Gulf Islands. Guides knowledgeable with conditions, tides, and area. Fully equipped new Necky kayaks. Introductory course for beginners. Lessons. Transport to and from ferry. Beachfront launching, parking. Kayaking and lodging packages for guests staying at Sutil Lodge. Individual or group rates. 250-539-5390. Fax: 250-539-5390.

Diving

Galiano Island Diving Service: Diving instruction. Boat diving. Wolf eels and ship-wrecks to view. Diving charters to Active and Porlier passes. Airfills and repairs. Located at Madrona Resort. 250-539-3109 or 250-539-5186.

Viable Marine Services: Pick-up and return for passengers from/to Mayne, Galiano, and Pender islands. Carries bikes and kayaks on boat. 250-539-3200. Fax: 250-539-3200.

Watercraft rentals

Ben's Gulf Island Kayaking: Sea kayak and canoe rentals. 250-539-2442.

Galiano Island Sea Kayaking: Kayak rentals and tours. 250-539-5390.

Montague Harbour Marina: Sea kayaks and boat rentals. 250-539-5733.

Bodega Ridge.

Charters

Bert's Charters: Year-round salmon fishing charters. 250-539-3181.

Catamaran Nature Sail and Gourmet Picnic: Sail the 46-foot catamaran *Great White Cloud* through the Gulf Islands. Explore islets, parks, and wildlife sanctuaries. Swim and walk on the beach. Gourmet lunches and group rates. 250-539-5390. Fax: 250-539-5390.

Dionisio Point Park Express: Leave from the government dock on the north end of the island. Travel through Porlier Pass and view the lighthouses. Land at Coon Bay in Dionisio Point Provincial Park. Sandy beach, warm water swimming lagoon. Coast Guard-approved water taxi with 10-person capacity. Schedule changes seasonally. 250-539-5186 or 250-539-3109.

Mel-n-I Charters: Luxury 32-foot Fairline. Maximum eight people. Children welcome. Fish and/or cruise the Gulf Islands, leaving from Sturdies Bay on Galiano Island. 250-539-3171. Fax: 250-539-3171.

Picnic spots

The public parks are ideal for picnics. As well, there are endless possibilities for picnicking in scenic spots all over the island: rocky outcroppings, beaches, public docks.

Golf

Galiano Golf and Country Club: On St. Andrew's Drive just off Ellis and Linklater roads. A 3871-yard course. Nine holes plus two extras allow for a different route on the return trip. Open to the public. Breakfast, lunch, snacks. Licensed restaurant. 250-539-5533.

Horseback riding

Bodega Resort: one- or two-hour trail rides. 250-539-2677.

Places to visit and things to see

Galleries

Art and Soul Craft Gallery: 2540 Sturdies Bay Road (just up the road from the ferry terminal). Galiano and B.C. artists' arts and crafts. Paintings, woodwork, pottery, silk, weaving, aromatherapy products, candles, and much more. 250-539-2944.

Dandelion Gallery: Just a few steps from the ferry terminal (first street on the left). A charming spot run by local artisans. Beautiful silk scarves, jewelry, paintings, sculpture, and much more. 250-539-5622.

Spotlight Studio: 20625 Porlier Pass Road. Studio filled with high-quality handmade items—paintings, clothes, household items by local artisans. 250-539-2294.

Other special spots

Ixchel Craft Shop: 61 Georgeson Bay Road at the junction with Sturdies Bay Road. Crafts by local and international artisans. Pottery, jewelry, musical instruments. 250-539-3038.

Kiln Glass Studio: 654 Burrill Road. Fused and cast glass. Open every day during July and August, weekends remainder of the year. 250-539-5004.

The Blue Goose Country Kitchen: 85 McClure Road (mid-island, on Porlier Pass Road). Crafts and home-made preserves. Some preserves feature wild fruit harvested from local forests. Handmade soaps. 250-539-2516.

The Camas Shop: 90 Active Pass Drive. Handcrafts, weaving, and pottery by island artisans. Watch for the sign. 250-539-2458.

Schoenfeld Custom Knives: 139 Warbler Road South. Quality handmade knives for camping, fishing, hunting. Knives for the kitchen and the collector. 250-539-2806.

What on Earth: 654 Burrill Road. Flower pots, cement figures, fountains and bird baths, Indonesian folk art, African baskets. 250-539-5004.

Watch along the roadside for pottery and craft sales signs—one of the treats of driving or cycling in the Gulf Islands.

Services

Churches and religions
Baha'i Faith 250-539-3361
St. Margaret of Scotland Anglican Church on Burrill Road
Roman Catholic Church at St. Margaret of Scotland Anglican Church on Burrill Road 250-539-3051

Cycle rental and repair
Ben's Bikes (bike rentals, no repairs done) 250-539-2442
Galiano Bicycle Rental and Repair (mountain bike rentals, basic repair) 250-539-9906

Fishing supplies and licenses
The Corner Store at Georgeson Bay and Sturdies Bay roads 250-539-2986
Montague Harbour Marina at Montague Harbour 250-539-5733
Sturdies Bay Gas & Groceries 250-539-5500

Grocery stores
Galiano Trading Company at 217 Sturdies Bay Road 250-539-5529
Daystar Market at the junction of Sturdies Bay and Georgeson Bay roads 250-539-2502
Montague Marina Store at Montague Harbour 250-539-5733
Sturdies Bay Gas & Groceries on your left about one short block from the ferry terminal 250-539-5500
The Corner Store at Sturdies Bay and Georgeson Bay roads 250-539-2986

Launching sites
see map on pages 75–77

Liquor store
The Corner Store at the corner of Sturdies Bay, Georgeson Bay, and Porlier Pass roads 250-539-2986

Marine repair
Montague Harbour Marina 250-539-5733

Medical
Galiano Health Care Centre at 908 Burrill Road 250-539-3230

Pay telephones
Montague Harbour Marina 250-539-5733

Post office
In the Daystar Market at the junction of Sturdies Bay and Georgeson Bay roads 250-539-2502

Public transportation
Go Galiano Island Shuttle (year-round bus/taxi/charter; ferry, B&B, and restaurant pick-up and delivery; reduced service in winter) 250-539-0202
Hummingbird Pub bus (runs between Montague Harbour and the pub, from late May to late September) 250-539-5472
Inter Island Launch Water Taxi 250-656-8788 or 250-383-4884
Viable Marine Services (pick-up and return for passengers from/to Mayne, Galiano, and Pender; bikes and kayaks allowed on boat) 250-539-3200 Fax: 250-539-3200

Conglomerate Rocks in Active Pass.

Public washrooms
Ferry terminal

Travel InfoCentre
Booth on your right just after you leave the ferry terminal (open daily in July and August and on weekends in May and June) 250-539-2233

Video rental
Daystar Market (specializes in foreign and art films) 250-539-2502

View from Mount Galiano.

Access by Boat

Government docks

Porlier Pass: First government dock on your left as you come out of the pass. Close to take-out food, bait, groceries, and pay phone.

Montague Harbour: On the southwest side of the island. Beautiful, naturally protected harbour near provincial park and camping facilities. Hiking trails on the ocean and through the forest. Home of Montague Harbour Marina. Two bed and breakfasts nearby.

Retreat Cove: Midway along the west side of the island. Secluded spot with dock and swimming.

Sturdies Bay (where the ferry docks): Short walk to the commercial centre on the island.

Whaler Bay: Near Sturdies Bay ferry terminal on the southern tip of the island. Easy walking to all facilities.

Marinas

Montague Harbour Marina: Overnight moorage, store, fuel, pay phone, marine supplies, limited repairs. Sea kayak rentals. Tackle and licenses. Montague gift shop with Galiano Island crafts. Licensed premises. Access to Montague Harbour Park. Pick-up point for Hummingbird Pub bus. 250-539-5733. VHF 68.

Loop routes

Short loop

After leaving the ferry by car or bike, turn left at the gas station and stop to browse in the Dandelion Gallery. This co-operative is an excellent source of handcrafted items such as silk blouses and scarves, earrings, and paintings. Chat with an artisan and learn about crafts on the island and island life.

Proceed a short distance along Sturdies Bay Road to Burrill Road, left onto Jack Road, and to Bellhouse Park. Stroll along the rocky shoreline and pause to watch bald eagles roost and ferries sail by.

Dandelion Gallery and Bellhouse Park can be visited easily on foot from the ferry terminal.

Return to Burrill Road and, at the turn where it becomes Bluff Road, pull over to savour the view of marine traffic in Active Pass. Continue on to explore Bluffs Park, a densely wooded area with trails, secluded spots, and a magnificent viewpoint high

Trollers leaving Whaler Bay, Galiano Island.

on a hill overlooking Active Pass. Follow Bluff Road through the park, turn right onto Georgeson Bay Road, and, at the intersection of Georgeson Bay, Porlier Pass and Sturdies Bay roads, stop for delicious food and a genuine pub ambience at the Hummingbird Pub or cross the road to Daystar Café with its regular and vegetarian menus, espresso bar, and indoor and outdoor dining. Cross the road to the Corner Store with the Ixchel Craft Shop stocked with work by local and international artisans. From here, it is an easy five minutes by car to the ferry terminal.

Longer loop

After stopping at Bluff Park, turn right on Georgeson Bay Road and left on Montague

Harbour Road to Montague Harbour Park. The park has a beautiful bay, picnic and camping sites, two shell beaches, hiking trails, and a magnificent view of the harbour and surrounding shoreline.

Backtrack to a dinner at La Berengerie, nestled in the trees at the junction of Montague Harbour and Clanton roads. This cozy inn caters to lovers of fine food.

Return to Porlier Pass Road and travel through an area with a wealth of views to the north end of the island. Turn left off Porlier Pass Road at Retreat Cove Road for some beachcombing—explore tidal pools and count starfish hiding in cracks and under rocks. Sit on the red government wharf and look out on the channel and islands.

Stop at Spotlight Studio at 20625 Porlier Pass Road and browse among the many locally crafted items.

Continue north to where the road turns away from the water. Then, return back down Porlier Pass Road toward the ferry, watching for the signs for Blue Goose Country Kitchen on McClure Road and Cedar Grove Pottery. From here, it is a short distance down Porlier Pass Road to the ferry.

Ferry seen from Bellhouse Park.

Special events

Galiano Weavers' and Spinners' Sale: Late June or early July. In the South Community Hall on Sturdies Bay Road.

North Galiano Jamboree: July 1st. At the North Galiano Community Hall.

Fiesta Day: On the B.C. Day long weekend in August. In the fairgrounds on Burrill Road. Annual Summer Fair with parade, pancake breakfast, barbecue.

Galiano Island Wine Festival: In August. At the Lions' Park Centre.

Blackberry Festival: On the Canadian Thanksgiving weekend (in October). At the Southend Hall on Sturdies Bay Road. Blackberry pie, blackberry tea, and more.

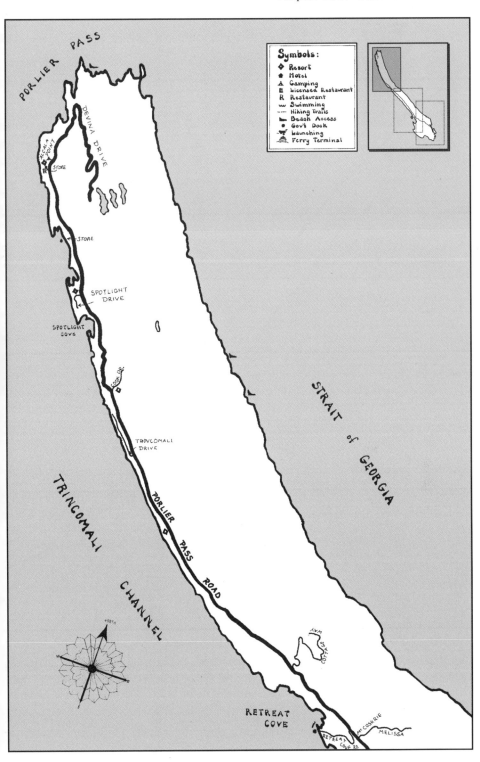

Symbols:
◆ Resort
♠ Motel
▲ Camping
Ⓛ Licensed Restaurant
R Restaurant
〰 Swimming
--- Hiking Trails
◣ Beach Access
● Gov't Dock
⚓ Launching
⛴ Ferry Terminal

PORLIER PASS

DEVINA DRIVE

STORE

STORE

SPOTLIGHT DRIVE

SPOTLIGHT COVE

STRAIT of GEORGIA

TRINCOMALI DRIVE

TRINCOMALI CHANNEL

PORLIER PASS ROAD

NORTH

RETREAT COVE

RETREAT COVE RD

MC COSKRIE

MELISSA

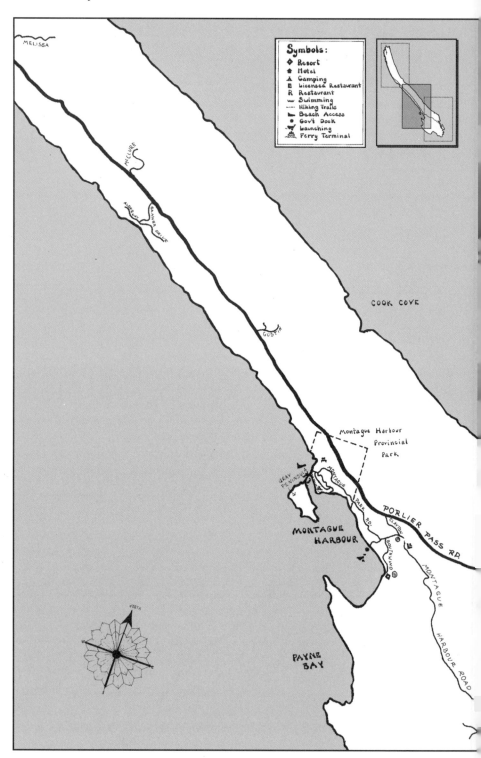

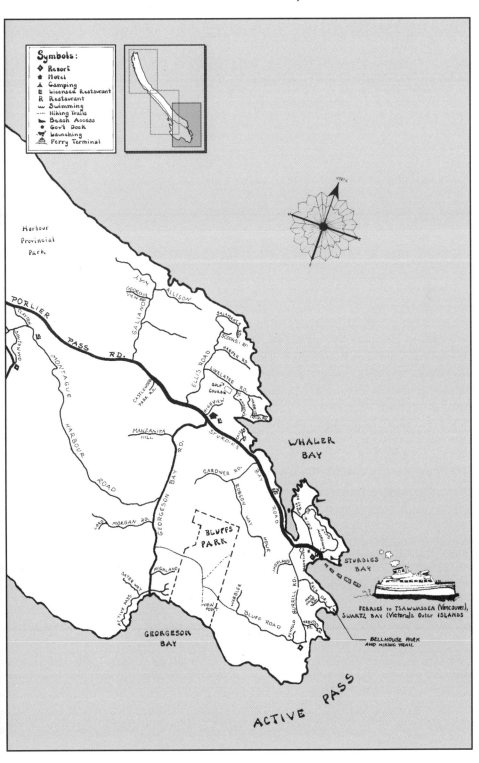

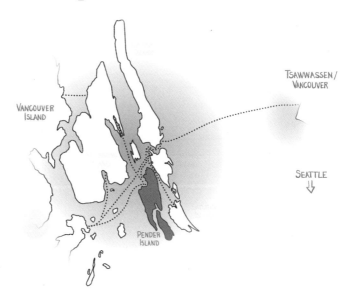

Chapter Three

North and South Pender Islands

*tranquillity • rustic charm • quiet country atmosphere • seascape views
• hiking • cycling • kayaking and canoeing • ocean swimming • lake
swimming • beachcombing • picnic spots • boat charters • scuba diving
• golfing • tennis • government docks • marinas • boaters' port of entry
with waterside lounge and pool • divers' lodge • galleries • fall fair •
historic store • farmers' market • resorts • lodges • inns • bed and
breakfasts • campgrounds • restaurants • pubs*

North and South Pender Islands, connected by a small bridge, lie to the south of
Galiano Island. The population of the two islands is about 1500. South Pender is the
smaller and less developed of the two. Many of the houses are concentrated on the
southwest side of North Pender Island, in sheltered settings where deer graze and
where there are captivating views of Swanson Channel.

Getting to North and South Pender by ferry

Getting to North and South Pender from the B.C. mainland by B.C. Ferries
1. From Tsawwassen to Otter Bay on North Pender Island: This is the most direct route from the mainland to Pender Island. Tsawwassen is 37 kilometres (about forty minutes) southwest of Vancouver on Highway 17. Sailing times vary from an hour and a half to two and a half hours, depending on the number of stops. Check the schedule for details. Reservations taken. Food service.

Ferry in Active Pass enroute to Pender Island.

2. From Tsawwassen to Swartz Bay on Vancouver Island and from Swartz Bay to Otter Bay on North Pender Island: Sailing times vary from two hours to three and a half hours depending on the number of stops. Check the schedule for details. Ask the cashier for a transfer. No reservations taken. Food service.
3. From Horseshoe Bay to Departure Bay (Nanaimo) on Vancouver Island, from Departure Bay to Swartz Bay, and from Swartz Bay to Otter Bay on North Pender Island: Horseshoe Bay is 23 kilometres (about thirty-five minutes) north of Vancouver. Sailing time from Horseshoe Bay to Departure Bay is about an hour and a half. From Nanaimo drive 132 kilometres (about two and a half hours) south to Swartz Bay and take the ferry to Otter Bay on North Pender Island. Sailing times to Otter Bay vary depending on the number of stops. Check the schedule for details. Reservations are taken on the Horseshoe Bay to Departure Bay route. Food service on both routes.

Getting to North and South Pender from Vancouver Island by B.C. Ferries
From Swartz Bay to Otter Bay on North Pender Island: Swartz Bay is on Vancouver Island 30 kilometres (forty-five minutes) north of Victoria. Sailing time varies depending on the number of stops. No reservations taken. Food service.

B.C. Ferries schedule information and reservations
British Columbia Ferries
1112 Fort Street
Victoria, BC V8V 4V2
Web site: http://www.bcferries.bc.ca
In British Columbia: 1-888-223-3779
Outside British Columbia: 250-386-3431

Getting to North and South Pender from the United States
1. From Tsawwassen, B.C. by B.C. Ferries: Drive to Tsawwassen, B.C., 230 kilometres north of Seattle, on Interstate Highway 5 and, in Canada, Highways 99 and 17. Sail directly to Otter Bay on North Pender Island (sailing times vary depending on the number of stops) or sail from Tsawwassen to Swartz Bay on Vancouver Island (sailing time is one and a half hours) and then transfer to the ferry going to Otter Bay on North Pender Island (sailing time is forty minutes). Reservations taken Tsawwassen to Pender. No reservations taken Swartz Bay to Pender. Food service Tsawwassen to Pender.

B.C. Ferries schedule information and reservations
British Columbia Ferries
1112 Fort Street
Victoria, BC V8V 4V2
Web site: http://www.bcferries.bc.ca
In British Columbia: 1-888-223-3779
Outside British Columbia: 250-386-3431
    B.C. Ferries accepts Visa and MasterCard for reservations and Visa, MasterCard, and Canadian and American currency at check-in. There are ATM machines and a currency exchange at the Tsawwassen terminal.

2. From Anacortes, Washington, by Washington State ferry system: Drive to Anacortes (85 miles north and 20 miles west of Seattle) and sail to Sidney, B.C. Sailing time is three hours. Reservations taken. Food service. From Sidney, drive 8 kilometres (fifteen minutes) to the B.C. Ferries terminal at Swartz Bay and catch the ferry to Otter Bay on North Pender Island. Sailing time is forty minutes.

Washington State Ferries schedule information and reservations
Washington State Ferries
Pier 52
801 Alaskan Way
Seattle, WA 98104-1487
E-mail: wsf@wsdot.wa.gov
Web site: http://www.wsdot.wa.gov/ferries/
In U.S.: 1-800-843-3779
Outside U.S.: 206-464-6400

Whales off Pender Island.

3. From Seattle, Washington by the Princess Marguerite (Clipper Navigation): Sail from Seattle to Victoria, B.C. Sailing time is four and a half hours. Reservations taken. Food service. From Victoria, drive 30 kilometres (forty-five minutes) to the B.C. Ferries terminal at Swartz Bay and take the ferry to Otter Bay on North Pender Island. Sailing time is forty minutes.

Clipper Navigation schedule information and reservations
Clipper Navigation
2701 Alaskan Way
Pier 69
Seattle, WA 98121
E-mail: clipper@nwlink.com
Web site: http://www.victoriaclipper.com/
In U.S.: 1-800-888-2535
Outside U.S.: 206-448-5000

4. From Port Angeles, Washington (on the Olympic Peninsula) by Black Ball Transport ferry: Drive to Port Angeles and sail on the Black Ball Transport ferry to Victoria, B.C. Sailing time is one and a half hours. No reservations taken. Food service. From Victoria, drive 30 kilometres (forty-five minutes) to the B.C. Ferries terminal at Swartz Bay and take the ferry to North Pender Island. Sailing time is forty minutes.

Black Ball Transport ferry schedule information and reservations
Black Ball Transport
430 Belleville Street
Victoria, BC V8V 1W9
Web site: http://www.northolympic.com/coho
In U.S.: 360-457-4491
In Canada: 250-386-2202

Accommodation

Plan ahead for accommodation because the limited facilities are heavily booked in the summer and may be closed in the off-season. There are no restaurants on the premises unless otherwise stated in the listings. The accommodations are on North Pender Island unless otherwise stated.

Other Resources

Pender Island Tourist Information Centre: On the left side of Otter Bay Road a few minutes' drive from the ferry terminal. (No phone service available.)

Canadian Gulf Islands Reservation Service
637 Southwind Road
Galiano Island, BC V0N 1P0
250-539-5390 Fax: 250-539-5390
E-mail: reservations@gulfislands.com
Web site: http://www.multimedia.bcit.bc.ca/b&b

British Columbia Bed and Breakfast Association
101—1001 West Broadway
Vancouver, BC V6H 4V1
604-734-3486 Fax: 604-985-6037

Island Escapades Adventures
118 Natalie Lane
Ganges, BC V8K 2C6
250-537-2537 Fax: 250-537-2532

Ministry of Tourism
Travel Reservation and Information Service
In Greater Vancouver: 663-6000
In North America, outside Greater Vancouver: 1-800-663-6000
Outside North America: 250-387-1642
Web site: http://www.tbc.gov.bc.ca/tourism/information.html

Resorts, lodges, inns

Bedwell Harbour Island Resort: 9801 Spalding Road. At Bedwell Harbour on South

Pender Island. Motel rooms, cottages, luxury townhouses. One- and two-bedroom units. Fireplaces, kitchens, water views, balconies. Licensed restaurant with indoor and outdoor dining. Marine bar and bistro. Heated outdoor pool. Tennis and volley-ball courts. Bike, canoe, boat rentals. Fishing charters and licenses. Meeting room. Customs Office for boaters entering Canada. 1-800-663-2899 in Canada and U.S. or 250-629-3212. Fax: 250-629-6777. VHF 68.
E-mail: bedwell@islandnet.com
Web site: http://www.islandnet.com/~bedwell/

Sh-qu-ala Inn: On Hamilton Road at Port Browning Marina. Cabins, camping, show-ers, laundromat. Tennis courts, pool, store, launching ramp. Licensed restaurant, pub, beer and wine store. 250-629-3493.

Pender Lodge: 1329 MacKinnon Road. Walking distance from the ferry. Four tranquil oceanfront acres. Panoramic views. Outdoor pool and tennis court. Fully equipped housekeeping cottages in park-like setting. Close to marina, boat and bike rentals, and restaurant. 250-629-3221.

The Inn on Pender Island: 4709 Canal Road. Secluded setting on seven acres adjacent to Prior Centennial Park. Nine rooms with queen-sized beds, cable TV, full ensuite bathrooms, private entrances, sun decks. Smoking and non-smoking rooms. Hot tub. Memories at the Inn restaurant on the premises. Wheelchair accessible. 250-629-3353. Fax: 250-629-3167.

Bed and breakfasts

These engaging establishments have a good range of prices. Call ahead to reserve—the demand for accommodation is high. Fliers are available on the racks on the British Columbia ferries. Also, check the large information board on your right after leaving the ferry.

Some bed and breakfasts open year-round:

Arbutus Retreat: 1105 Ogden Road. Peaceful retreat in a woodland setting. One unit, private suite with antique brass double bed. Sea view from deck. Ground floor, no stairs. Gourmet breakfast cooked by the authors of *The Pender Palette* and *A Food History To Victoria*. 250-629-2047.

Beauty Rest By The Sea: 1301 McKinnon Road. Five acres at waterfront on a penin-sula. Panoramic waterfront views. Serene surroundings. Two ensuite bedrooms with private entrances. Coffee and fridge in each room. Full breakfast. Cruises available. 250-629-3855. Fax: 250-629-3856.

Camelot by the Sea: 1215 Otter Bay Road. Waterfront Victorian manor, private sandy beach, ocean views, sunsets, ferry and marine traffic, wildlife. All suites overlook the water. One self-contained, very private suite with fireplace accommodates two to four people. Walking distance to sandy beach, ferry, golf course. 250-629-3770.

Honeymoon suite, Cliffside Inn on-the-sea.

Cliffside Inn on-the-sea: 4230 Armadale Road. Three kilometres from the ferry. Oceanfront setting with mile-long beach overlooking Mount Baker and Navy Channel. Private sessions in cliffhanger hot tub. Candlelight, fireside dining (for guests only). Four suites with private baths, two with fireplaces. 250-629-6691.

Eatenton House: 4705 Scarff Road. Secluded forest-edge location with ocean views. Guest sitting room with fireplace and antiques. Garden sun deck. 250-629-8355.

Hummingbird Hollow: 36125 Galleon Way. Lakeside suites with fridges, private baths, lakeview sunrooms, balconies. Common room with woodstove. Gourmet breakfast. Country garden. Close to ocean and trails. Bird watchers' and nature lovers' paradise. No stairs. 250-629-6392.

Whale-Cum-Inn: 2602 Harpoon Road. Three acres on the oceanfront at Shingle Bay. Deck views of sunsets and ferries. Dock, canoes, trampolines. Three bedrooms with baths. Large homemade breakfast of fruits, cheeses, cinnamon buns. 250-629-6525.

Campgrounds

Prior Centennial Provincial Park: On Canal Road near Port Browning and Bedwell Harbour. Seventeen sites for vehicle or tent camping. Two beaches—Hamilton and Medicine—within walking distance. Trail and lookout over Port Browning. Closed approximately November through February.

Beaumont Marine Park: On South Pender Island at Bedwell Harbour. Accessible on foot or by water only. Good mooring and anchorage. Ten walk-in campsites.

Sh-qu-ala Inn: At Port Browning. Camping. Licensed restaurant, pub, beer and wine store. 250-629-3493.

Dog Tooth Violet.

Restaurants, pubs, and take-out food

Bedwell Harbour Island Resort: 9801 Spalding Road on South Pender Island. Follow Canal and Spalding roads to Bedwell Harbour. Spacious dining room and lounge on the harbour at the boat customs. Bar and bistro. Indoor and outdoor dining. Licensed. 250-629-3212.

Village Bakery: In the Driftwood Centre at Bedwell Harbour and Razor Point roads. Homemade soups and breads. Build your own sandwiches. Mini pizza, cappuccino, many delicious breads, buns, desserts. 250-629-6453.

Memories at the Inn: 4709 Canal Road. At the Inn on Pender Island, near Prior Centennial Park. Country cooking. Memorabilia from the forties, fifties, and sixties is mixed with oak, brass, and etched glass. Licensed. 250-629-3353.

The Poplars: 1325 MacKinnon Road on North Pender Island. Fine dining—duck, lamb, veal, chicken, fresh seafood. Open for dinner every night. Outside and inside dining. Patio overlooking ocean. Licensed. Closed October through April. 250-629-3955.

Fairways Café: At the golf course on Grimmer Road near Grimmer Bay. Home-cooked breakfasts and lunches all week, Sunday brunch. Licensed. 250-629-6665.

Sh-qu-ala Inn and Lodge: At Port Browning Marina. Neighbourhood pub and café overlooking the bay. Family dining in a cozy room with beamed ceiling and fireplace. Licensed. 250-629-3493.

The Stand: At the ferry terminal. Breakfast, lunch, and supper. Seafood, burgers, and milkshakes. Outside tables and take-out. 250-629-3292.

Take-out food

Memories at the Inn: Country cooking. 250-629-3353.

Village Bakery in Driftwood Centre: Soups, sandwiches, breads, desserts. 250-629-6453.

The Stand at the ferry terminal: Seafood, burgers, milkshakes. 250-629-3292.

Activities

Cycling

Both North and South Pender provide pleasant cycling on easy routes along tree-lined roads with ocean views. The Loop Route section provides suggestions for a tour around the islands.

Cycling supplies, rentals, repairs
Otter Bay Marina: Bicycle rentals. 250-629-3579.

Hiking

Mount Norman Park: Access on Ainslie Road, South Pender Island, just beyond the bridge where North and South Pender join. Access on foot only. Panoramic view reached by moderate difficulty trail.

Beaumont Marine Park: Adjacent to Mount Norman Park. Access on foot at the bridge where North and South Pender join or by water in Bedwell Harbour.

Many trails are on private land although many have been hiked by the public for years. Ask at the InfoCentre for information on accessing the trails. The Magic Lakes area of North Pender has many trails in small parks dotted throughout the area.

Swimming and beach access

Bridges Road at Wiley Point: At the north end of North Pender Island.

Harpoon Road at Shingle Bay: On the west side of North Pender Island.

Thieves Bay: On the west side of North Pender Island.

Hamilton Beach: In Browning Harbour on North Pender Island.

Medicine Beach: In Bedwell Harbour on South Pender Island.

Craddock Drive: Near Tilley Point on South Pender Island.

Gowlland Point: On the south-east tip of South Pender Island.

Kayaking and canoeing

Cooper's Landing: Kayak charters. Video available describing lodge and services. 250-629-6133.

Mouat Point Kayaks: At Otter Bay Marina. Kayak tours, lessons. 250-629-3579.

Raccoon.

Diving

Tilly Point: On the south side of South Pender Island. Popular diving area noted for underwater caves.

Cooper's Landing: Diving lodge, two boat dives per day, air compressors. Minimum six people in a group. Call first for reservations. Kayak charters for registered guests.

Video available describing lodge and services. 250-629-6133.

Viable Marine Services: Diving services. Owners are licensed skippers and qualified divers (PADI). 250-539-3200. Fax: 250-539-3200.

Watercraft rentals

Bedwell Harbour Resort: Canoe, kayak, and boat rentals. 250-629-3212.

Otter Bay Marina. Kayak and powerboat rentals. 250-629-3579.

Charters

Cooper's Landing: Diving and kayak charters for registered guests. 250-629-6133.

Eagle Spirit Charters: 21-foot fully equipped Campion. Fishing, exploring. Pick-up at Miners Bay, Mayne Island; Sturdies Bay, Galiano Island; and Port Washington Dock, North Pender Island. 250-539-5540.

Mouat Point Kayaks: At Otter Bay Marina. Guided tours. Beginners welcome. Hidden bays, secluded beaches, seal covered islands, marine life. All tours begin with orientation on kayaking skills and safety procedures. 250-629-6767. E-mail: tilley@horizon.bc.ca

Picnic spots

Thieves Bay Park and Shingle Bay Park on the west side of North Pender Island.

Prior Centennial Park off Canal Road on North Pender Island.

Golf

Public golf course on Grimmer Road, North Pender Island. Nine holes on 2341 yards. Golf club and power car rentals. Fully stocked pro shop. Licensed lounge and restaurant. 250-629-6659.

Tennis

On Privateers' Road, North Pender Island.

Places to visit and things to see

Galleries

(All on North Pender Island except Simpson Studios)

Fern-green gallery: 4510 Bedwell Harbour Road. Family gallery. Paintings, photography, country crafts. 250-629-3523.

Galloping Moon Gallery: At the wharf at Hope Bay, junction of Hope Bay Road and Clam Bay Road. Featuring works by over fifty local artists. Paintings, pottery, fiber arts, jewelry, clothing, drums, carvings and more. Open every day June through September. 250-629-6020.

Hummingbird Studio and Gallery: 7903 Swanson View Drive near Wallace Point. Home studio and gallery. Original stained glass art, panels, watercolour images. Commissions considered. 250-629-6596.

Joyful Symmetry Country Crafts: 3309 Port Washington Road. Herb and floral designs studio filled with fragrant dried flowers, wreaths, topiaries, herbal creations from their gardens and orchard, stoneware, table and bed linens. 250-629-6476.

Ruffed Grouse.

Margaret Grimmer Gallery: 2301 Otter Bay Road. Abstract and landscape watercolours of the islands. Handmade driftwood lamps. Also the home of Gulf Island Seeds, locally and organically grown wild and native flower and herb seeds. Watch for the "Gallery Open" sign on Otter Bay Road near Grimmer Road. 250-629-3373.

Pender Island Crafts: On Aldridge Road, next to AT's store. Handcrafted works, pottery, knitting, and more by island craftspeople.

The Armstrong Gallery: 1201 Otter Bay Road. Oil paintings and watercolours by the owners. Maritime subjects, birds, and wildlife. 250-629-6571.

Renaissance Studios: 3302 Port Washington Road. Quality custom jewelry from bohemian crystal beads, antiques, oriental rugs, art, and art restoration. 250-629-3070.

Simpson Gallery and Studios: 9978 Gowlland Point Road on South Pender Island. Watch for the sign. Artist's working studio. Original paintings. Island images, small to large in oil and acrylic. Represented by galleries in Western Canada and the U.S. Commissions accepted. 250-629-6512.

The Wool Shed: 4312 Clam Bay Road. Homespun wool items. Weaving, sweaters and socks, woven blankets, and baskets. Dyed silk scarves. Homemade wood items.

Services

The Driftwood Centre, at the junction of Bedwell Harbour, Razor Point, and Canal Roads is the main spot for goods and services.

Banks
Hongkong Bank of Canada at the Driftwood Centre 250-629-6516

Car rental
Local Motion 250-629-3366

Churches and religions
Church of the Good Shepherd (Anglican) on South Pender Island 250-629-3312
United Community Church 250-629-3822
Roman Catholic Church 250-629-3141
St. Peter's Anglican Church on North Pender Island 250-629-3634

Cycle rental and repair
Bedwell Harbor Resort at Bedwell Harbour (rentals only) 250-629-3212
Otter Bay Marina off MacKinnon Road at Otter Bay (rentals only) 250-629-3579

Drugstore
Pender Pharmacy at the Driftwood Centre 250-629-6555

Fishing supplies and licenses
Otter Bay Marina off MacKinnon Road on Otter Bay, North Pender Island (licenses, bait, supplies) 250-629-3579

Grocery stores
AT General Store at 5827 Schooner Way at Aldridge and Wallace roads 250-629-5114
Southridge Farm Country Store at 3327 Port Washington Road 250-629-2051
The Grocery Store at the Driftwood Centre

Launching sites
see map on pages 96-99

Laundromats
Bedwell Harbour Resort and Marina 250-629-3212
The Driftwood Centre

Otter Bay Marina 250-629-3579
Port Browning Marina 250-629-3493

Library
4407 Bedwell Harbour Road 250-629-3722

Liquor stores
The Driftwood Centre 250-629-3413
Beer and Wine Store at Port Browning Marina 250-629-3493

Marine repair
Sabyan Auto Marine Repair (shop and mobile unit; serves marinas at Otter Bay, Bedwell Harbour, Browning Bay, and Thieves Bay; specializes in emergency repairs) 250-629-3240
Seastar Marine at 37162 Galleon Way (certified marine technician; 24-hour emergency service 7 days per week; mobile unit serves all marinas on North and South Pender; access to all marine parts) 250-629-3680

Medical clinic
5715 Canal Road 250-629-3233

Pay telephones
Tourist Information Centre on Otter Bay Road
Bedwell Harbour Resort and Marina
The Driftwood Centre
Otter Bay Marina
AT General store at Aldridge and Wallace roads
Medical Centre at Aldridge and Canal roads
Ferry terminal

Post office
The Driftwood Centre 250-629-3222

Public transportation
Pender Taxi 250-629-9900
Inter Island Launch Water Taxi 250-656-8788 or 250-383-4884
Viable Marine Services (pick-up and return for passengers from/to Mayne, Galiano, and Pender; bikes and kayaks allowed on boat) 250-539-3200 Fax: 250-539-3200

Public washrooms
Ferry terminal

RCMP
250-629-6171

Showers
Bedwell Harbour Resort and Marina 250-629-3212
Otter Bay Marina 250-629-3579

Access by boat

Government docks

Brackett Cove: Port Browning. Marina, wharf, moorage (reservations accepted), laundromat, showers, store, beer and wine store, Sh-qu-ala Inn with restaurant and pub, outdoor swimming pool and tennis courts, launching ramp.

Bedwell Harbour: resort and marina with groceries, licensed restaurant and lounge, fuel, pay phone, laundromat, Canada Customs.

Grimmer Bay: northwest end of North Pender Island.

Hope Bay: northeast end of North Pender Island.

Port Washington: northwest end of North Pender Island.

Razor Point Road at Browning Harbour: southeast side of North Pender Island.

Marinas

Bedwell Harbour Island Resort and Marina: Bedwell Harbour, South Pender Island. One-hundred-twenty-slip marina with fuel and fishing licenses. Showers, laundromat, motel rooms, cottages, restaurant, bistro, indoor and outdoor dining, heated pool, licensed lounge, store. Canoe and bike rentals. Customs office for boaters entering Canada. 250-629-3212

Otter Bay Marina: Otter Bay, North Pender Island. Five-minute walk from ferry terminal. Cabin rental (sleeps four to five). Store, pay phone, laundromat, showers, swimming pool, covered picnic tables, large outdoor fireplace, overnight moorage, launching ramp; kayak, powerboat, and bike rentals. Fishing licenses and supplies. Cappuccino, island crafts, clothing. Marina is open year round, store open mid-May to fall. 250-629-3579

Loop route

After leaving the ferry, go north on Otter Bay Road toward Grimmer Bay, watching for the Armstrong Gallery at 1201 Otter Bay Road, where there are original oil paintings and watercolours by the owners. At the Margaret Grimmer Gallery at 2301 Otter Bay Road, there are paintings, driftwood lamps, and organically grown wildflower and herb seeds.

Go east to 3302 Port Washington Road to Renaissance studios with handcrafted glass bead jewelry, antiques, and art.

Joyful Symmetry, at 3309 Port Washington Road, is a delightful herb and floral designs studio filled with fragrant dried flowers, wreaths, topiaries, and herbal creations from their gardens and orchard, stoneware, and table and bed linens.

Continue on down Port Washington Road to Southridge Farms Country Store where you will find ice cream, groceries and general supplies, organic vegetables, and hikers' mixes.

Then go on to Hope Bay Heritage Store at the junction of Hope Bay and Clam Bay roads. This heritage building, built in 1905, has an eclectic supply of ethnic clothing, jewelry, novelties, crafts, and new and used books. Sandwiches, cappuccino, and ice cream are available at oceanside tables.

The Goldsmith Shop nearby has custom-made jewelry and a variety of stones and old coins. Galloping Moon Gallery has works by over fifty local artists, paintings, pottery, fiber arts, jewelry, clothing, drums, carvings, and more.

If you are looking for an outstanding bed and breakfast, try Cliffside Inn on-the-sea, a captivating spot in an unforgettable location (see the section on bed and breakfasts).

Take Clam Bay Road to The Wool Shed at 4312 Clam Bay Road where you will find homespun wool items, weaving, handmade sweaters and socks, woven blankets and baskets, dyed silk scarves and handmade wood items. They are open every day from May 1 through September 30.

Continue south on Bedwell Harbour Road stopping at Fern-green Gallery at 4510 Bedwell Harbour Road. This family gallery features paintings, photography, and country crafts.

Continue a short way to the Driftwood Centre, Pender's commercial centre. Village Bakery offers baked goods, homemade soups, pizza, decadent desserts, and cappuccino. On Saturday mornings, May to October, you will find the Farmers' Market here.

Continue south on Canal Road. Turn left onto Hamilton Road to Port Browning Marina and Sh-qu-ala Inn with its licensed restaurant, pub, camping, and resort.

Return to Canal Road and relax at Prior Centennial Park, a secluded area with picnic spots and campsites. Enjoy country cooking at Memories at the Inn Restaurant at the Inn on Pender Island, near Prior Centennial Park. Forties, fifties, and sixties memorabilia mix with oak, brass, and etched glass in a relaxed setting.

Follow Canal Road across the bridge to South Pender Island and enjoy the drive through densely wooded areas along Boundary Pass Drive.

Double back to the junction of Boundary Pass and Spalding roads. Turn left and follow the road to Bedwell Harbour Island Resort. Have a snack, meal, or refreshing drink indoors or out. Vacationers checking in at customs add a feeling of festivity to

is waterside restaurant and shop surrounded by flowers, an outdoor pool, and boats
f all kinds.
Travel on toward Gowlland Point, watching for Simpson Gallery and Studios at
980 Gowlland Point Road. Stop in to see their original paintings of island images.
Continue on to the public beach access at Gowlland Point. Beachcomb and relax on
is stretch of beach with wide open views across Boundary Passage to the San Juans.

pecial events

armers' Market: Every Saturday, May to October. At the Driftwood Centre at the
nction of Bedwell Harbour, Razor Point, and Canal roads.

all Fair: Late August. At Hastings Field next to the Driftwood Centre.

ope Bay Store.

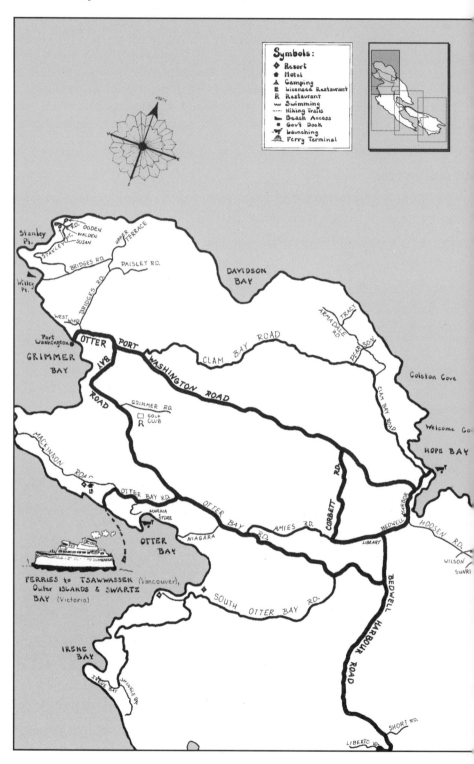

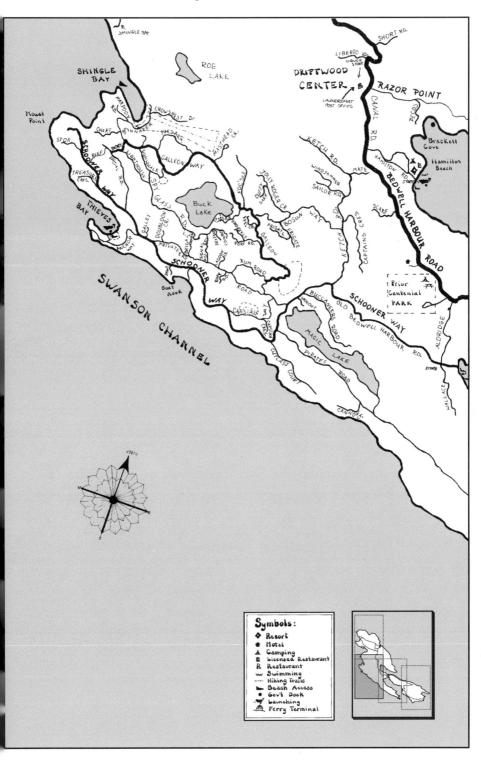

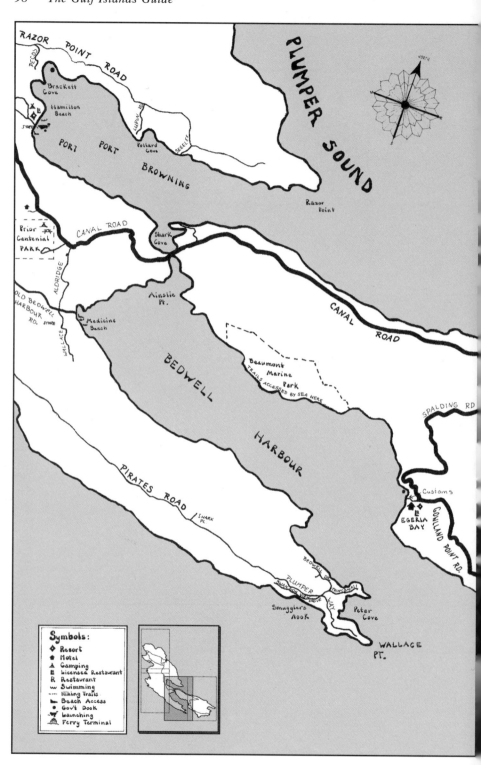

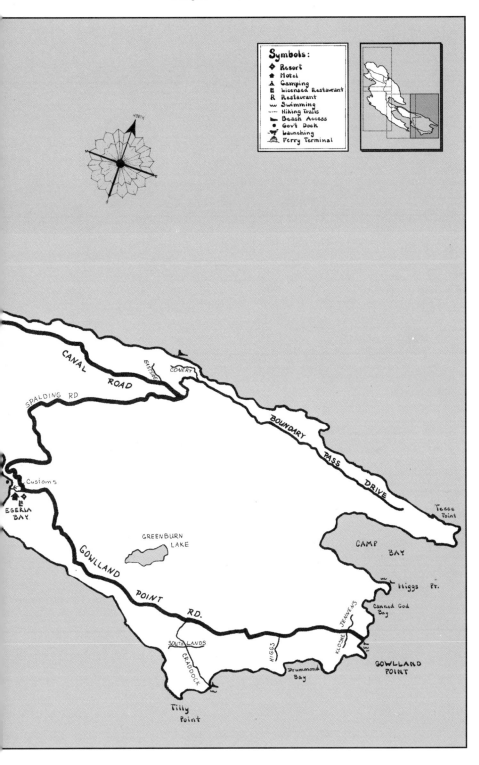

Chapter Four

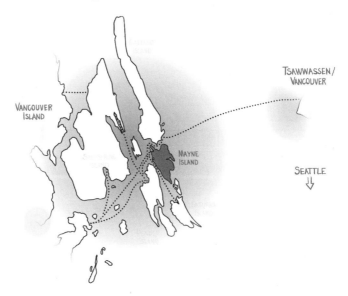

Mayne Island

tranquillity • rustic charm • quiet country atmosphere • seascape views • hiking • cycling • kayaking and canoeing • ocean swimming • beachcombing • picnic spots • boat charters • scuba diving • tennis • government docks • galleries • lightstation • museum • salmon derby • fall fair • Christmas craft fair • old-fashioned general store • resorts • lodges • inns • bed and breakfasts • campgrounds • restaurants • pubs

The population of Mayne Island is about 800. Many of the houses on the island date from the early 1900s and add immensely to the charm of their surroundings. There is a pleasant sensation of open lawns and neighbourliness mixed with heavily treed, untouched areas.

Getting to Mayne by ferry

Getting to Mayne from the B.C. mainland by B.C. Ferries
1. From Tsawwassen to Village Bay on Mayne Island: This is the most direct route from the mainland to Mayne Island. Tsawwassen is 37 kilometres (about forty

minutes) southwest of Vancouver on Highway 17. Sailing times vary from an hour to an hour and a half depending on the number of stops. Reservations taken. Food service.

2. From Tsawwassen to Swartz Bay on Vancouver Island and from Swartz Bay to Village Bay on Mayne Island: The total sailing time varies between two hours and three and a half hours, depending on the number of stops. Ask the cashier for a transfer. No reservations taken. Food service.

3. From Horseshoe Bay to Departure Bay (Nanaimo) on Vancouver Island, from Departure Bay to Swartz Bay, and from Swartz Bay to Village Bay on Mayne Island: Horseshoe Bay is 23 kilometres (about thirty-five minutes) north of Vancouver. Sailing time from Horseshoe Bay to Departure Bay is about an hour and a half. From Nanaimo drive 132 kilometres (about two and a half hours) south to Swartz Bay and take the ferry to Village Bay on Mayne Island. Sailing times to Village Bay vary depending on the number of stops. Reservations taken on the Horseshoe Bay to Departure Bay route. Food service.

Getting to Mayne from Vancouver Island by B.C. Ferries
From Swartz Bay to Village Bay on Mayne Island: Swartz Bay is on Vancouver Island 30 kilometres (forty-five minutes) north of Victoria. Sailing times vary depending on the number of stops. No reservations taken. No food service.

B.C. Ferries schedule information and reservations
British Columbia Ferries
1112 Fort Street
Victoria, BC V8V 4V2
Web site: http://www.bcferries.bc.ca
In British Columbia: 1-888-223-3779
Outside British Columbia: 250-386-3431

Getting to Mayne from the United States
1. From Tsawwassen, B.C., by B.C. Ferries: Drive to Tsawwassen, B.C., 230 kilometres north of Seattle, on Interstate Highway 5 and, in Canada, Highways 99 and 17. Sail directly to Village Bay on Mayne Island (sailing times vary depending on the number of stops) or sail from Tsawwassen to Swartz Bay on Vancouver Island (one and a half hours) and then transfer to the ferry to Village Bay on Mayne Island. Reservations taken Tsawwassen to Mayne. No reservations taken Swartz Bay to Mayne. Food service Tsawwassen to Mayne.

B.C. Ferries schedule information and reservations
British Columbia Ferries
1112 Fort Street
Victoria, BC V8V 4V2
Web site: http://www.bcferries.bc.ca
In British Columbia: 1-888-223-3779
Outside British Columbia: 250-386-3431

B.C. Ferries accepts Visa and MasterCard for reservations and Visa, MasterCard, and Canadian and American currency at check-in. There are ATM machines and a currency exchange at the Tsawwassen terminal.

2. From Anacortes, Washington by Washington State ferry system: Drive to Anacortes (85 miles north and 20 miles west of Seattle) and sail to Sidney, B.C. Sailing time is three hours. Reservations taken. Food service. From Sidney, drive 8 kilometres (fifteen minutes) to the B.C. Ferry terminal at Swartz Bay and catch the ferry to Village Bay on Mayne Island. Sailing times vary depending on the number of stops.

Washington State Ferries schedule information and reservations
Washington State Ferries
Pier 52
801 Alaskan Way
Seattle, WA 98104-1487
E-mail: wsf@wsdot.wa.gov
Web site: http://www.wsdot.wa.gov/ferries/
In U.S.: 1-800-843-3779
Outside U.S.: 206-464-6400

3. From Seattle, Washington by the Princess Marguerite (Clipper Navigation): Sail from Seattle to Victoria, B.C. Sailing time is four and a half hours. Reservations taken. Food service. From Victoria, drive 30 kilometres (forty-five minutes) to the B.C. Ferries terminal at Swartz Bay and take the ferry to Village Bay on Mayne Island. Sailing times vary depending on the number of stops.

Clipper Navigation schedule information and reservations
Clipper Navigation
2701 Alaskan Way
Pier 69
Seattle, WA 98121
E-mail: clipper@nwlink.com
Web site: http://www.victoriaclipper.com/
In U.S.: 1-800-888-2535
Outside U.S.: 206-448-5000

Toadstools.

4. From Port Angeles, Washington (on the Olympic Peninsula) by Black Ball Transport ferry: Drive to Port Angeles and sail on the Black Ball Transport ferry to Victoria, B.C. Sailing time is one and a half hours. No reservations taken. Food service. From Victoria, drive 30 kilometres (forty-five minutes) to the B.C. Ferries terminal at Swartz Bay and take the ferry to Village Bay on Mayne Island. Sailing times vary depending on the number of stops.

Black Ball Transport ferry schedule information and reservations
Black Ball Transport
430 Belleville St.
Victoria, BC V8V 1W9
Web site: http://www.northolympic.com/coho
In U.S.: 360-457-4491
In Canada: 250-386-2202

Accommodation

Accommodations are quite limited. There are no public camping facilities on Mayne Island. There is no Travel InfoCentre on Mayne Island. The Chamber of Commerce may be contacted by writing to P.O. Box 160, Mayne Island, B.C. V0N 2J0 (no phone service available).

Other resources

Canadian Gulf Islands Reservation Service
637 Southwind Road
Galiano Island, BC V0N 1P0
250-539-5390 Fax: 250-539-5390
E-mail: reservations@gulfislands.com
Web site: http://www.multimedia.bcit.bc.ca/b&b

British Columbia Bed and Breakfast Association
101—1001 West Broadway
Vancouver, BC V6H 4V1
604-734-3486 Fax: 604-985-6037

Island Escapades Adventures
118 Natalie Lane
Ganges, BC V8K 2C6
250-537-2537 Fax: 250-537-2532

Ministry of Tourism
Travel Reservation and Information Service
In Greater Vancouver: 663-6000
In North America, outside Greater Vancouver: 1-800-663-6000
Outside North America: 250-387-1642
Web site: http://www.tbc.gov.bc.ca/tourism/information.html

Resorts, lodges, inns

There are no restaurants on the premises in the following listings unless mentioned.

Blue Vista Resort: 563 Arbutus Drive. Tranquil park-like setting. One- and two-bedroom cabins with fireplaces, fully equipped kitchens, barbecues, sun decks, and bicycles. Near tennis, beach, hiking, and swimming. 250-539-2463.

Fernhill Lodge: 610 Fernhill Road. Bed and breakfast lodge with emphasis on providing a haven from city life. Separate units decorated with historical themes. Private baths. Some hot tubs. Sauna. Breakfast included. Dinners by reservation. Gourmet food (historical or modern menus). Licensed. 250-539-2544.

Mayne Inn: On Bennett Bay at the end of Bennett Bay Road. Oceanfront rooms with queen-sized beds and private baths. Sandy beach. Fireside lounge, meeting room facilities. Family restaurant. Licensed. 250-539-3122. Fax 250-539-5119.

Oceanwood Country Inn: 630 Dinner Bay Road. Waterfront. Ten acres overlooking Navy Channel. Twelve guest rooms, each with bathroom. Eight rooms with fireplaces and whirlpool baths or large soaking tubs. Private decks facing the ocean. Sauna, oceanfront hot tub, library, living room, games room, bicycles for guests. Breakfast and tea included. Licensed restaurant specializing in in-season, locally-oriented cuisine and West Coast wines. Conference facilities for twelve, with meeting supplies. Group rates. 250-539-5074. Fax: 250-539-3002.

Springwater Lodge: At Fernhill and Village Bay roads in Miners Bay. Built in the 1890s, is British Columbia's oldest continuously operating hotel. At the government dock overlooking Active Pass. Fully modern, self-contained two-bedroom beachfront cabins with kitchens and sun decks. Sleeping rooms with shared baths in the lodge. Superb views of passing ferries and other marine traffic. Lunch and dinner served in the lounge or on the deck. 250-539-5521.

Bed and breakfasts

The Chamber of Commerce prints an annual flier listing island facilities, including bed and breakfasts. It is available on the ferries or by writing Mayne Island Community Chamber of Commerce Box 160, Mayne Island, B.C. V0N 2J0.

Some bed and breakfasts open year-round are:

Fernhill Lodge: 610 Fernhill Road. Emphasis on providing a refuge from everyday life. An historical theme pervades the lodge with rooms and meals linked to various stages in history. Gourmet dining specializing in original Roman, Medieval, and Renaissance recipes with herbs from the hosts' extensive garden. Sunday brunch. Licensed. 250-539-2544.

Mayne Inn: On Bennett Bay at the end of Bennett Bay Road. Oceanfront rooms, sandy beach, fireside lounge, meeting room facilities. Family restaurant. Licensed. 250-539-3122. Fax: 250-539-5119.

The Root Seller Inn: 478 Village Bay Road. Large heritage house overlooking Active Pass. Group prices for cyclists, hikers, and families. Hearty buffet breakfasts. 250-539-2621.

Campgrounds

There are no public campgrounds on Mayne Island.

Fern Hollow Campground: 640 Horton Bay Road. Eight private, secluded campsites. Covered cooking area. Hot showers. No RVs. Eight kilometres from ferry terminal. Fifteen-minute walk from Horton Bay. 250-539-5253

Restaurants, pubs, and take-out food

Fernhill Lodge: 610 Fernhill Road. Gourmet dining, including Sunday brunch. Imaginative cuisine specializing in Roman, Medieval, and Renaissance dinners drawn from original recipes and containing fresh herbs from the extensive garden. Licensed. 250-539-2544.

Mayne Inn: On Bennett Bay at the end of Bennett Bay Road. Oceanfront dining in family restaurant. Pub with fireplace. Licensed. 250-539-3122.

Mayne Mast Restaurant: On Village Bay Road at the junction of Fernhill Road and Miners Bay Road. Home-cooked meals. Licensed. 250-539-3056.

Oceanwood Country Inn: 630 Dinner Bay Road. Award-winning Northwest cuisine. Dinner served daily, brunch on Saturdays and Sundays. Reservations recommended. Licensed. 250-539-5074.

Springwater Lodge.

Springwater Lodge: Dockside at Miners Bay. Pub, dining room, and deck dining at an historic lodge. Great views of ferries and marine traffic passing close by. Licensed. 250-539-5521.

Take-out food

Manna Bakery: Bakery and café on Village Bay Road near Fernhill Road. 250-539-2323.

Activities

Cycling

Roads on Mayne Island are fairly flat, but they are often narrow and winding with both paved and gravel surfaces.

See the Loop Route section for a recommended route.

Cycling supplies, rentals, repairs
Georgina Point Bicycle Repair: Repairs only. 250-539-2598.

Hiking

Many trails are in a natural state. Watch for drop-offs and other potential hazards. Take time to savour the many beautiful spots and use the beach accesses. See the Loop Route section for suggestions.

Swimming and beach access

Bennett Bay: At the end of Bennett Drive.

Bennett Bay: Off Klippen and Arbutus at Paddon Point.

Campbell Bay: Off Waugh Road.

Dinner Bay Park: Off Dinner Bay Road south of Village Bay Georgina Point.

Lightstation: Off Waugh Road at Georgina Point.

Miners Bay: At Village Bay and Fernhill roads near Springwater Lodge.

Oyster Bay: North side.
Piggott Bay: South side.

Gallagher Bay, Mayne Island.

Kayaking and canoeing

Mayne Island Kayak and Canoe Rentals: 359 Maple Drive. Canoes, single and double kayaks. Tours of Mayne Island and overnight tours to other islands. All equipment provided. Instruction for beginners and up. Rescue instruction. Equipment, marine charts, kayaking books sales. Camping, hot tub, and outdoor shower for kayakers and canoeists. Complimentary ferry pick-up and drop-off. 250-539-2667.

Diving

Turtle Island Dive Adventures: Instruction. Dive and boat charters. Shore and orientation dives. 250-539-2437.

Viable Marine Services: Diving services. Owners are licensed skippers and qualified divers (PADI). 250-539-3200. Fax: 250-539-3200.

Watercraft rentals

Mayne Island Kayak and Canoe Rentals. At the foot of Maple Drive on Seal Beach. Kayak and canoe rentals, instruction, and sales. Ferry pick up and drop off. 250-539-2667.

Charters

Island Charters: Half-day or full-day sailing, sightseeing, fishing cruises in the Gulf Islands on a 33-foot cruising sailboat. Pick-up and drop-off can be arranged on other islands. 250-539-5040.

Picnic spots

Dinner Bay Park: Follow Dalton Drive and Dinner Bay roads south from the ferry. Community park on eleven acres at Dinner Bay. Picnic tables, cookhouse, barbecue, electricity, running water, public washrooms, horseshoe pits. Wheelchair accessible.

Tennis

On Felix Jack Drive behind the firehall. Open daily.

Places to visit and things to see

Galleries

The Artery: 508 Bayview Drive (near Oyster Bay). Paintings, prints, and collages by Frances Faminow and associated artists. Workshops arranged for all ages. Noon to 5 p.m. daily; winter hours as posted. 250-539-2835.

Charterhouse Country Crafts: Watch for the sign on Charter Road at Bennett Bay. Home studio of Heather Maxey. Quilts and fine woollens processed from her sheep. 250-539-2028.

John Charowsky Studio and Gallery: 490 Fernhill Road at Campbell Bay Road Walking distance from Miners Bay. Functional pottery and porcelain. One-of-a-kind pieces. Located in a serene wooded setting. Open 10 a.m. to 5 p.m. daily. Closed Wednesday. Reduced hours in off-season. 250-539-3488.

Larry Holbrook: Paintings of the Gulf Islands, particularly of Mayne Island and marine birds. Watercolour, acrylic, and oil. Commissions undertaken. By appointment only. 250-539-2414.

Historical sites

Active Pass Lightstation: Off Georgina Point Road at the north end of the island. The original lighthouse was built on this site in 1885 and replaced by the present lightstation in 1940. Spacious grounds on the seashore. Open to the public during seasonal hours posted at the gate.

Mayne Museum: On Fernhill Road just east of the Trading Post. Originally the building was the Plumper Pass Lock-up, a jail built in the late 1800s and used during the gold rush. Native artifacts, settlers' tools, and photos. Open July through August and by appointment. 250-539-5286.

Services

Cycle rental and repair
Georgina Point Bicycle Repair (repairs only) 250-539-2598

Churches and religions
St. Mary Magdalene (Anglican) on Georgina Point Road
Chapel of St. Francis of Assisi (Catholic) at 313 Mariner's Way

Fishing supplies and licenses
Active Pass Auto and Marine on Fernhill Road 250-539-5411

Grocery stores
Mayne Open Market (MOM's) at 574 Fernhill Road (delivery service to home or boat) 250-539-5024
Miners Bay Trading Post at junction of Village Bay Road and Fernhill Road 250-539-2214
Tru Value Foods in Maynestreet Mall on Village Bay Road near Fernhill Road

Health centre
At 466 Felix Jack Road 250-539-2312

Launching sites
see map on pages 114-115
David Cove
Piggott Bay
Village Bay

Liquor store
At Miners Bay Trading Post 250-539-2214

Marine repair
Active Pass Auto and Marine at Miners Bay (marine repair and fuel dock service)
250-539-5411
Active Pass Repairs (mobile unit) 250-539-5971

Pay telephones
Miners Bay Trading Post
Ferry terminal
Maynestreet Mall

Trading Post, Mayne Island.

Post office
On Village Bay Road at Miners Bay 250-539-5024

Propane
Active Pass Auto and Marine on Fernhill Road near Montrose 250-539-5411

Public transportation
Inter Island Launch Water Taxi 250-656-8788 or 250-383-4884
Mayne Island Taxi (ferry pick-up, can carry two bikes) 250-539-3439
Viable Marine Services (pick-up and return for passengers from/to Mayne, Galiano,
and Pender; bikes and kayaks allowed on boat) 250-539-3200 Fax: 250-539-3200

Public washrooms
Dinner Bay Park
Ferry terminal

Access by boat

Government docks
Horton Bay: No facilities, good anchorage.
Miners Bay: Access to the Trading Post and Tru Value Foods for groceries, supplies, liquor, pay phones, post office, restaurants, and pub.

Loop route

From the ferry terminal, follow Village Bay Road through the ferns and firs to the Maynestreet Mall on your right. Check the Chamber of Commerce fliers on display here for information on the island.

The Trading Post General Store, a few steps away and a feature of island life for many years, is cozy and well stocked. Pick up the local papers, the Mayne Liner and Island Tides, to really tune in to island life.

Mayne Museum.

Stop at the museum on Fernhill Road just up the road from the Trading Post. Browse among Native artifacts, settlers' tools, and photos in this authentic relic of older days—the museum, built in 1896, was the jail during gold rush days.

Return to Fernhill Road, turn left onto Campbell Bay Road, which later becomes Waugh Road, and right onto Georgina Point Road to the Active Pass Lightstation.

This scenic point looking onto Active Pass is the site of the original lighthouse, which was built in 1885. The current lightstation was built in 1940, and the new tower in 1969. The grounds are open to visitors as posted on the sign at the gate. There is easy access to the rocky shoreline. Snowcapped mountains on the mainland, Galiano Island, and passing ferries make this a superb picture and picnic spot.

Once you decide to start back, return a short distance along Georgina Point Road, turn left onto Bayview Drive and watch for the sign for the Artery. This gallery features paintings, prints, and collages by Frances Faminow and associated artists. Open hours are noon to 5 p.m. daily; winter hours as posted.

Take a walk along the beach at Oyster Bay if the tide allows. The public beach access is near Georgina Point.

Afterwards, take Georgina Point Road toward Miners Bay. Stop for refreshments on the deck of Springwater Lodge. This vantage point is ideal for watching ferries, fishing boats, and pleasure boats make their way through Active Pass.

If you are looking for an unforgettable dining and lodging experience, call for reservations at Fernhill Lodge bed and breakfast. Secluded in the woods, this is a tranquil hide-away with a unique emphasis—an historical theme flows through the rooms and the menus. They prepare Roman, Medieval, and Renaissance dishes from original recipes, using herbs grown at the lodge. Cordial hosts add the finishing touches to make this a truly memorable stop.

Set out along Fernhill Road again, continuing straight ahead until you reach the T at the water. Turn right onto Arbutus Drive and right again onto Charter Road to visit Charterhouse Country Crafts. Watch for the sign on Charter Road at Bennett Bay. This is the home studio of Heather Maxey, who makes quilts and woolens with wool from her sheep.

Double back along Arbutus Drive to Bennett Bay for a swim or a walk on the beach. Find the beach access by going to the left on Wilkes Road and then right on the unnamed access road.

For a pleasant trip along island roads, head for Dinner Bay Park with its picnic tables and barbecues on the bay.

Special events

Mayne Island Canada Day Celebrations: July 1st. At Dinner Bay Park.

Springwater Salmon Derby: second weekend in August. Outdoor barbecue, prizes. At Springwater Lodge in Miners Bay.

Fall Fair: second Saturday in August.

Lions' Annual Salmon Bake: Labour Day Sunday (September).

Christmas Craft Fair: last weekend in November.

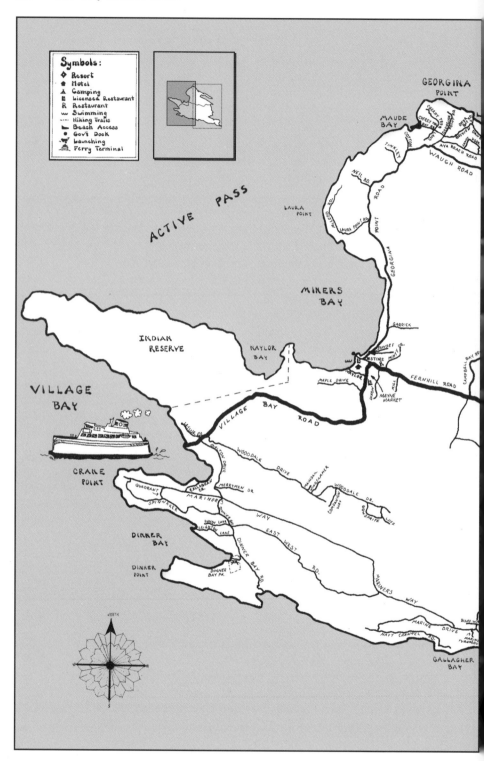

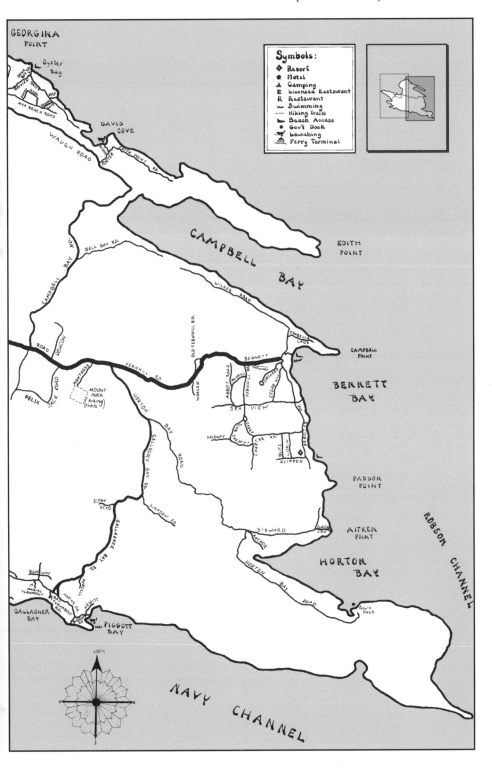

Chapter Five

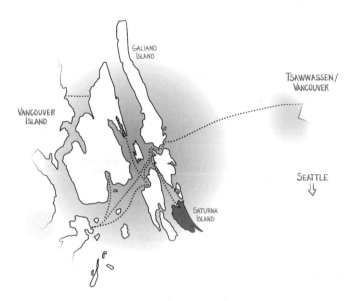

Saturna Island

least developed of all the islands • tranquillity • rustic charm • quiet country atmosphere • seascape views • hiking • cycling • kayaking and canoeing • ocean swimming • beachcombing • picnic spots • boat charters • scuba diving • government docks • galleries • farm bakery • resorts • lodges • restaurants • pubs

Saturna's charm lies in its isolation and tranquillity. There are entrancing coves and beaches along the rocky, unsettled coastline and the seclusion provides a pervasive sense of time slowed down.

Getting to Saturna by ferry

Getting to Saturna from the B.C. mainland by B.C. Ferries

1. From Tsawwassen to Village Bay on Mayne Island and from Village Bay to Lyall Harbour on Saturna Island: This is the most direct route from the mainland to Saturna Island. Tsawwassen is 37 kilometres (about forty minutes) southwest of Vancouver on

Highway 17. Sailing time from Tsawwassen to Village Bay varies from an hour to an hour and a half, depending on the number of stops. Check the schedule for details. Ask the cashier for a transfer. Reservations taken and food service on the Tsawwassen to Village Bay route. Sailing times from Village Bay on Mayne Island to Lyall Harbour on Saturna Island vary.

2. From Tsawwassen to Swartz Bay on Vancouver Island and from Swartz Bay to Lyall Harbour on Saturna Island: Sailing time from Tsawwassen to Swartz Bay is about an hour and a half. Sailing time from Swartz Bay to Lyall Harbour varies depending on the number of stops. Check the schedule for details. Ask the cashier for a transfer. No reservations taken. No food service.

Getting to Saturna from Vancouver Island by B.C. Ferries
1. Swartz Bay to Lyall Harbour on Saturna Island: Swartz Bay is on Vancouver Island 30 kilometres (forty-five minutes) north of Victoria. Sailing time varies depending on the number of stops. Check the schedule for details. No reservations taken. No food service.

Saturna Island Ferry.

B.C. Ferries schedule information and reservations
British Columbia Ferries
1112 Fort Street
Victoria, BC V8V 4V2
Web site: http://www.bcferries.bc.ca
In British Columbia: 1-888-223-3779
Outside British Columbia: 250-386-3431

Getting to Saturna from the United States

1. From Tsawwassen, B.C. by B.C. Ferries: Drive to Tsawwassen, B.C., 230 kilometres north of Seattle, on Interstate Highway 5 and, in Canada, Highways 99 and 17. Sail from Tsawwassen to Village Bay on Mayne Island and from Village Bay to Lyall Harbour on Saturna Island, or sail from Tsawwassen to Swartz Bay on Vancouver Island (one and a half hours) and then transfer to the ferry to Lyall Harbour on Saturna Island. Reservations taken Tsawwassen to Saturna. No reservations taken Swartz Bay to Saturna. Food service Tsawwassen to Saturna.

B.C. Ferries schedule information and reservations
British Columbia Ferries
1112 Fort Street
Victoria, BC V8V 4V2
Web site: http://www.bcferries.bc.ca
In British Columbia: 1-888-223-3779
Outside British Columbia: 250-386-3431
   B.C. Ferries accepts Visa and MasterCard for reservations and Visa, MasterCard, and Canadian and American currency at check-in. There are ATM machines and a currency exchange at the Tsawwassen terminal.

2. From Anacortes, Washington by Washington State ferry system: Drive to Anacortes (85 miles north and 20 miles west of Seattle) and sail to Sidney, B.C. Sailing time is three hours. Reservations taken. Food service. From Sidney, drive 8 kilometres (fifteen minutes) to the B.C. Ferry terminal at Swartz Bay and catch the ferry to Lyall Harbour on Saturna Island. Sailing times from Swartz Bay to Lyall Harbour vary depending on the number of stops.

Washington State Ferries schedule information and reservations
Washington State Ferries
Pier 52
801 Alaskan Way
Seattle, WA 98104-1487
E-mail: wsf@wsdot.wa.gov
Web site: http://www.wsdot.wa.gov/ferries/
In U.S.: 1-800-843-3779
Outside U.S.: 206-464-6400

3. From Seattle, Washington by the Princess Marguerite (Clipper Navigation): Sail from Seattle to Victoria, B.C. Sailing time is four and a half hours. Reservations taken. Food service. From Victoria, drive 30 kilometres (forty-five minutes) to the B.C. Ferries terminal at Swartz Bay and take the ferry to Lyall Harbour on Saturna Island. Sailing times from Swartz Bay to Lyall Harbour vary depending on the number of stops.

Clipper Navigation schedule information and reservations
Clipper Navigation
2701 Alaskan Way
Pier 69
Seattle, WA 98121
E-mail: clipper@nwlink.com
Web site: http://www.victoriaclipper.com/
In U.S.: 1-800-888-2535
Outside U.S.: 206-448-5000

4. From Port Angeles, Washington (on the Olympic Peninsula) by Black Ball Transport ferry: Drive to Port Angeles and sail on the Black Ball Transport ferry to Victoria, B.C. Sailing time is one and a half hours. No reservations taken. Food service. From Victoria, drive 30 kilometres (forty-five minutes) to the B.C. Ferries terminal at Swartz Bay and take the ferry to Lyall Harbour on Saturna Island. Sailing times from Swartz Bay to Lyall Harbour vary depending on the number of stops.

Black Ball Transport ferry schedule information and reservations
Black Ball Transport
430 Belleville Street
Victoria, BC V8V 1W9
Web site: http://www.northolympic.com/coho
In U.S.: 360-457-4491
In Canada: 250-386-2202

Accommodation

Accommodation is extremely limited on Saturna. There are no public campgrounds.

Other resources

Canadian Gulf Islands Reservation Service
637 Southwind Road
Galiano Island, BC V0N 1P0
250-539-5390 Fax: 250-539-5390
E-mail: reservations@gulfislands.com
Web site: http://www.multimedia.bcit.bc.ca/b&b

British Columbia Bed and Breakfast Association
101—1001 West Broadway
Vancouver, BC V6H 4V1
604-734-3486 Fax: 604-985-6037

Island Escapades Adventures
118 Natalie Lane

Ganges, BC V8K 2C6
250-537-2537 Fax: 250-537-2532
Ministry of Tourism
Travel Reservation and Information Service
In Greater Vancouver: 663-6000
In North America, outside Greater Vancouver: 1-800-663-6000
Outside North America: 250-387-1642
Web site: http://www.tbc.gov.bc.ca/tourism/information.html

Resorts and Lodges

East Point Resort: 187 East Point Road. Six oceanside cottages in a parklike setting overlooking Tumbo Island and Georgia Strait. One- and two-bedroom cottages with equipped kitchens, baths, and decks with view. Sandy beach. Boat rentals and ramp. 250-539-2975.

Saturna Lodge: 130 Payne Road. Three right turns (five minutes' drive) from the Lyall Harbour ferry dock. Elegant, newly refurbished country inn overlooking Boot Cove. Seven rooms (single and double) with ocean and garden views, down quilts, original art, soaker tubs, private decks, terry robes. Two lounges with fireplaces. Fully licensed gourmet restaurant on premises. Accommodation rates include Continental breakfast. Can accommodate seminars, retreats, and business functions. Complimentary bus service to and from the ferry. 1-888-539-8800 in Canada and the U.S. or 250-539-2254. Fax: 250-539-3091.
E-mail: satlodge@gulfislands.com
Web site: http://www.gulfislands.com/saturna/satlodge

Stonehouse Farm Resort: 207 Narvaez Bay Road. Seventeenth-century-style farmhouse on twenty-five acres. Secluded waterfront setting on Narvaez Bay. Small farm with sheep and a highland cow. Private, sandy beach. Bedrooms with private baths and balconies. Ocean and Mount Baker views. One waterfront cottage with facilities for six. English farmhouse breakfast included. Shuffleboard, pool, darts. Boat available for fishing. Ferry pick-up with a vintage car. 250-539-2683. Fax: 250-539-2683.

Campgrounds

There are no camping facilities on Saturna Island.

Restaurants, pubs, and take-out food

Lighthouse Restaurant and Pub: At the ferry terminal in Lyall Harbour. Eat-in and take-out. Beautiful ocean view. Pool and darts. No minors. Licensed. 250-539-5725.

Saturna Lodge: 130 Payne Road at Boot Cove. Three right turns (five minutes' drive) from the ferry terminal. Fresh local seafood, Saturna Island lamb, organic garden produce, delicious desserts. Barbecues in summer. Licensed bar features award-winning

B.C. wines. Secluded setting. Restaurant deck overlooks the bay. Complimentary bus service from the ferry and from anchorage at Winter Cove. Tour the vineyard. 1-888-539-8800 or 250-539-2254.

Activities

Cycling

The roads are narrow and winding. However, traffic is lighter than on the other islands. East Point and Tumbo Channel roads make an easy and rewarding route with stretches of rocky beach right along the roadside.

Hiking

The only marked hiking trail is at Winter Cove Marine Park, an enticing setting with a short trail through the woods and along the water.

Diving

Viable Marine Services: Diving services. Owners are licensed skippers and qualified divers (PADI). 250-539-3200. Fax: 250-539-3200.

Swimming and beach access

East Point Road: Ruggedly beautiful rock beaches form the shoreline of the strait.

Charters

Viable Marine Services: Three-hour scenic and wildlife tours including Orcas. A 23-foot (10-passenger) boat and 24-foot (12-passenger) boat. Pick up and return for passengers from Mayne, Galiano, and Pender islands. Can carry bikes and kayaks on boat. Diving services. Owners are licensed skippers and qualified divers (PADI). 250-539-3200. Fax: 250-539-3200.

Picnic spots

Winter Cove Marine Park: North of the ferry terminal on Winter Cove. Picnic tables and old-fashioned, hand-operated water pump. This is the only designated public picnic site but many marvelous spots for an impromptu picnic exist around the island.

Places to visit and things to see

Gallery Rosa: 111 East Point Road. Woodturning, pottery, jewelry, and fine art. Short walk from dock and ferry. 250-539-2866.

Heron.

Shades of Saturna Gallery: 108 Payne Road at Boot Cove Road. Painting, pottery, weaving, woodwork, handmade jewelry by Saturna artists. 250-539-2559.

Haggis Farm Bakery: Just past the cemetery on Narvaez Bay Road—watch for the sign on the side of the building. Home-baked breads, cookies, cinnamon buns, croissants, English muffins. Pasta. Take-out pizza on Saturdays. All made with organic flour milled on the premises. 250-539-2591.

Services

Fishing supplies and licenses
Saturna Point Store at the ferry dock (licenses, tackle, bait) 250-539-5725

Grocery stores
Saturna General Store at Harris and Narvaez Bay roads 250-539-2936
Saturna Point Store at the ferry terminal 250-539-5725

Launching sites
see map on pages 126-127
Ferry terminal

Liquor store
Saturna General Store at the junction of Harris and Narvaez roads 250-539-2936

Pay telephones
Ferry terminal
East Point Lightstation

Post office
East Point Road near the ferry terminal 250-539-3233

Public washrooms
Winter Cove Marine Park

Public transportation
Inter Island Launch Water Taxi 250-656-8777 or 250-383-4884
Viable Marine Services (can carry bikes and kayaks inter-island) 250-539-3200

Access by boat

Government dock
At the Ferry Terminal in Lyall Harbour: Access to grocery store, fishing supplies, tackle, bait, fuel, pub and restaurant, take-out food, pay phone, post office.

Bald Eagle.

Loop route

Follow East Point Road to Winter Cove Road, turn left, and stop at Winter Cove Provincial Marine Park. Have a waterside picnic, drink some refreshingly cold water from the old-fashioned, hand-operated pump, and take a short hike on the marked trail. Poke around on the beach and soak up the silence.

Backtrack along Winter Cove Road. Continue straight ahead on East Point Road, following the picturesque tree-lined shore to long stretches of rocky beach perfect for beachcombing and relaxing. This road will take you to East Point and the lightstation grounds with public access to the water's edge—more chances for beachcombing and enjoying the view. Follow the rocks around the point and marvel at the sandstone sculptures carved by the waves.

Return to the ferry terminal in time for refreshments on the deck of the Lighthouse Restaurant where it is hard to take your eyes off the view. The setting is relaxing and the food filling in this island pub.

Special events

Lamb Barbecue: Canada Day (first weekend in July). At Winter Cove Marine Park, accessed by boat or by car. Annual event since 1949.

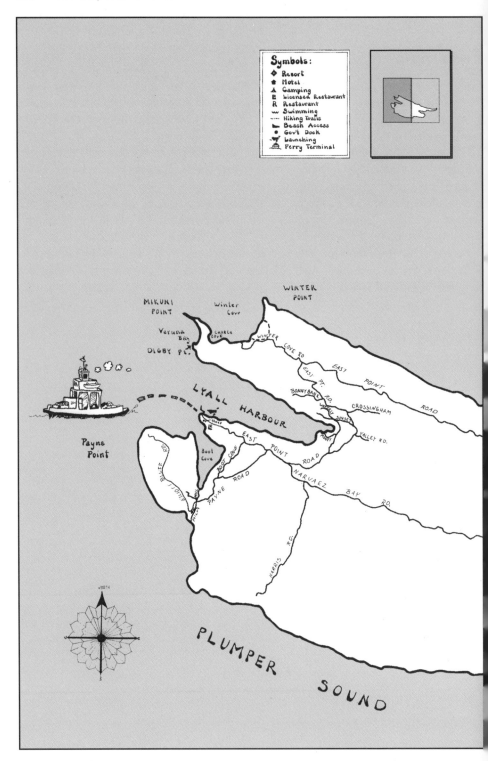

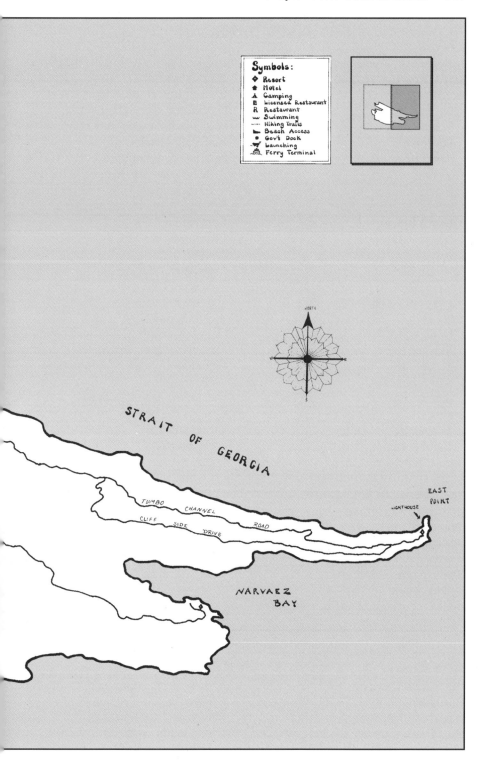

Symbols:
◇ Resort
♠ Motel
▲ Camping
ℝ Licensed Restaurant
R Restaurant
∿ Swimming
···· Hiking Trails
▶ Beach Access
● Gov't Dock
Launching
Ferry Terminal

NORTH

STRAIT OF GEORGIA

TUMBO CHANNEL

CLIFF SIDE DRIVE ROAD

LIGHTHOUSE

EAST POINT

NARVAEZ BAY

Index